12 - 30 - 85

THE MAKING OF A HERO

THE STORY OF LIEUT. WILLIAM CALLEY JR.

by Wayne Greenhaw

the reporter who first released
the My Lai story

First printing, June, 1971

Library of Congress Catalog Card Number: 79-166284

Printed in the United States of America

THE MAKING OF A HERO

a behind-the-scenes view of
the Lt. William Calley affair

by Wayne Greenhaw

Touchstone Publishing Company
Louisville, Kentucky

DEDICATION
Dedicated to the memory of
Sgt. Thomas Leland Hughes,
1941-1968.

WEATHER
Cloudy and mild with showers
day. Cloudy and cool tonight
d Thursday with chance of
in. High today, 73; l-w
night, 50; high Thursday, 65.
(More Weather, Page 2)

ALABAMA JOURNAL

FINAL
EDITION
FOR NEWS BULLETINS
DIAL 265-8246

81ST YEAR—NO. 271   MONTGOMERY, ALABAMA, WEDNESDAY AFTERNOON, NOVEMBER 12, 1969   36 PAGES   PRICE 10c

Ft. Benning Probes Vietnam Slayings

Officer Suspect In 91 Deaths Of Civilians

By WAYNE GREENHAW

A 26-year-old Army officer at Ft. Benning, Ga., is being investigated on charges of "the multiple murder of civilians in South Vietnam."

Informed sources told the **Journal** the officer is suspected of wiping out an entire South Vietnamese village by killing 91 people—men, women and children.

Lt. William L. Calley, an infantry officer, "has been told that allegations have been made against him," the public information officer at Ft. Benning said.

Col. Douglas B. Tucker said, however, that Calley was not under arrest and is not being confined to barracks.

After an Article 32 investigation under the uniform military code was made, Tucker said, "it took a stenographer about two weeks to transcribe the report."

The case, originally ordered by Calley's brigade commander, has not been referred to the commanding officer at Ft. Benning, Maj. Gen. Orwin C. Talbott.

"In complicated cases like this one, it may take a couple of weeks before the general gets the case," Tucker commented.

Calley, who lists his home town as Waynesville, N.C., joined the Army in July 1966 in Albuquerque, N.M. He was born in Miami.

The alleged slayings took place in March 1968, little more than a year after Calley arrived in South Vietnam.

The information officer at Ft. Benning told the **Journal** the office there got the case for investigation at the end of August this year.

If the case comes to trial it will be at Ft. Benning, Tucker said.

Under the military code, an Article 32 investigation is similar to a civilian grand jury. The investigation results in a recommendation to the appropriate authority as to whether there should be a court martial. Then authorities have to approve a trial, if one is to be held.

If the commanding general approves this trial, the information officer said, the case then goes to the judge advocate general, who will prepare the prosecution.

Defending Calley is civilian attorney George Lattimer of Salt Lake City, Utah. Lattimer is a retired judge on the Military Court of Appeals.

"An army has a personality. Beneath the individual thoughts and emotions of its component parts it thinks and feels as a unit. And in this large, inclusive sense of things lies a wiser wisdom than the mere sum of all that it knows."

—*Ambrose Bierce*
"One Kind of Soldier"

"It makes a difference whose ox is gored."
—Martin Luther

"Boys will be boys."
—*An attorney's comment*

"Only the dead have seen the end of war."

—*Plato*

"Lt. Price, it is not permitted for you to know anything. It is sufficient that you obey my orders."

—*Ambrose Bierce*
"One Kind of Soldier"

"Fuck the Vietnam War."

—*Lt. William L. Calley Jr.*

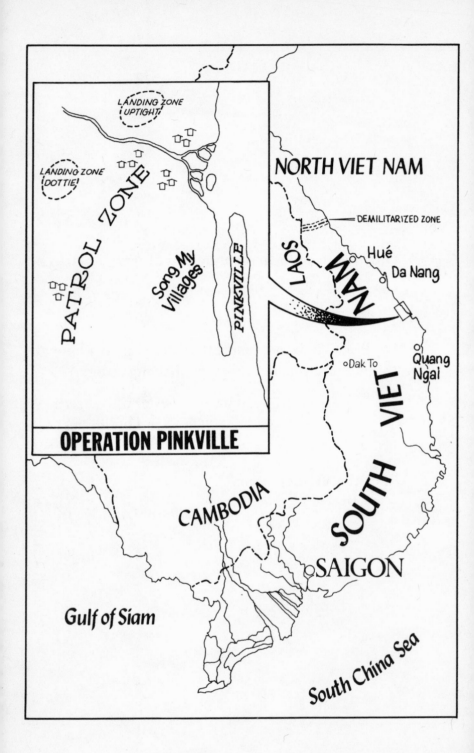

OPERATION PINKVILLE

LANDING ZONE UPTIGHT

LANDING ZONE DOTTIE

PATROL ZONE

Song My Villages

PINKVILLE

NORTH VIET NAM

DEMILITARIZED ZONE

LAOS

VIET NAM

Hué

Da Nang

Dak To

Quang Ngai

SOUTH VIET

CAMBODIA

SAIGON

Gulf of Siam

South China Sea

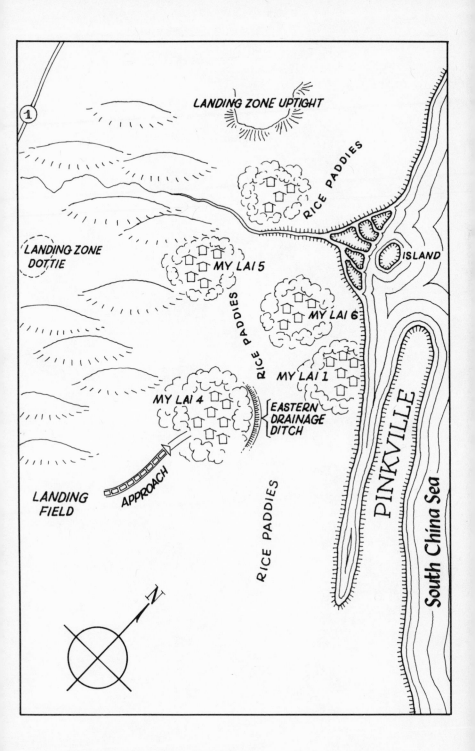

Table of Contents

Introduction

I have attempted to bring to you on the pages of *The Making of a Hero* all that I know about a story of a place, a happening and a people.

This has been no easy book to write, because it was begun in many, many different versions.

Originally, nearly two years ago, I planned to tell a dispassionate story, the tale as seen through the eyes of an objective journalist; but this has changed considerably.

If you want the facts and only the facts, do not go forward. Turn away and go elsewhere.

Primarily I give you the story of First Lt. William L. Calley and his emergence from a little man in a big army. In the eyes of many today he is a national hero. Why did he become a hero? And how did he become a hero?

I give you the story from my own viewpoint as well as from the eyes of others who were there. It's not a nice story, not a sweet story; most of the value judgments are my own. At the end of a long period of time, after knowing so many of the people involved, after feeling good and bad and sorrowful and hurt and other emotions, this is like opening an old wound; the pain is different, but it reminds one of the original ache.

No excuses are offered, and no promises; I lay myself bare for you to inspect, live with and judge for yourself.

Peace!

Wayne Greenhaw
West Egg Two
Destin, Florida

Chapter One

Limbo: I

Two boys, each five years old, stood in a field next to a busy street in Birmingham, Alabama.

Each wore a miniature helmet. Play-like belts of bullets hung loosely from their small bodies. In their hands were rifles patterned after the M1 of World War Two.

"My daddy was at Anzio," one said. The helmet tilted to one side, he was the serious braggadocio, puffed up with the knowledge that he was correct.

9

"Where's that?" the other asked.

The first kid's eyes squinted thoughtfully.

"Where?"

The first shrugged. "I don't know. Somewhere overseas, I think."

The other's father was somewhere with the U.S. Army, but he couldn't remember the name of the place. He backed away. Assuming a crouched position, he held his rifle alert. "The enemy's down by the creek," he whispered.

The first copied his stance and followed.

Each was careful to make little or no sound as their feet tiptoed across fallen leaves.

At a small embankment next to the trickle of water which cut through the suburban area they dropped to their knees.

No one was on the other side of the creek. All was silent except the sounds of traffic behind them. Nevertheless, they were extremely cautious. They were up against the most impossible of enemies: time. Somewhere in the future youth would disappear, but they didn't know it that day when their imaginations ran rampant on the empty lot in the Southern city.

"There they are," the first pointed out.

Each fixed his rifle to his shoulder. Each took aim at whatever his mind told him was present in the shrubbery across the way.

10

"Bam!" the first said.

"Bam! Bam!"

Their rapid fire continued until the twilight sound of a mother's call interrupted the war.

Even then, however, they didn't want to leave. They wanted to be free of the enemy. Each went through another round, firing as quickly as possible.

The call came more sharply from the back steps of a nearby house, and they knew they had to give up the fighting for the day.

Walking home, their rifles dangling in the hands, the first said, "I'm going to be a real soldier someday."

"Me too," said the other.

"I want to go somewhere far away and fight like my daddy's fighting."

The other nodded.

More than two decades later Sgt. Thomas Leland Hughes was blown beyond recognition in a city called Saigon when an unrecognizable enemy stepped out of an alleyway and threw a grenade to his feet.

The other member of the two-boy patrol sat in a newspaper office in Alabama and read about his friend being killed. I never made it to the war in Vietnam, never realized the ambition of a child's dream, and at that moment I felt sick that it had ever needed to be fulfilled by anyone.

11

War becomes totally destructive as a personal institution. It has no glory when the flag is ripped to shreds and is soaked in the blood of its youth. It has no right to exist when an entire nation is made to feel guilty for its sins.

And when the guilt takes over, the state of the nation is limbo. Webster defines limbo: the abode of souls barred from heaven through no fault of their own, esp. of the souls of just men who died before the coming of Christ, or of the souls of unbaptized infants; hence: a place of confinement, or a place or condition of neglect or oblivion.

Two months after my friend, Tommy Hughes, was killed by Vietcong in the massive Tet Offensive which ended with more than 10,000 American soldiers dying in ten days, a massacre of South Vietnamese took place in a little hamlet called My Lai Four.

At other places scattered throughout the area along the Ho Chi Minh Trail leading from North Vietnam supply headquarters into South Vietnam battle zones other mass killings of civilians took place. Perhaps none of them were as apparently bloody as the My Lai massacre, and it appears that none involved the large number of victims that My Lai took. Nevertheless, witnesses have described numerous killings of old men, women and children during the months which followed Tet.

"When the Cong made its first attack on Saigon, we didn't know what was taking place," said a black sergeant from Macon, Georgia, two years later.

Leon Morrison, a sharecropper's son who joined the Army to get away from the racial tensions of the South and "to gain a place of self-respect in everyman's Army," lost an arm and a leg during the first month of 1968.

"When the first explosions started we were as surprised as the people must have been at Pearl Harbor nearly 30 years ago. We lost our cool, and ole Charley came on us like you ain't ever seen. It was a rush that was as strong as anything I had ever seen in combat before.

"The first assault left us senseless. Our leaders didn't know what to do. Or at least that's the way I felt at the time. We were just out there in the middle of nowhere with nothing to do. We had our M16's and our grenades. But we were without direction.

"I was hit the first time during the second day of Tet. It was just a wound in the upper part of my arm. A medic fixed it. I could still fire my rifle. I didn't feel too good, but I knew we had to face up to whatever was happening.

"Believe me, when you had been safe as long as we thought we had been, sudden fire and explosions and shots out of nowhere scare the holy shit out of you. I'd have done anything to hold my position."

Morrison, who now attends a college within five miles of the south Georgia flatlands where his father cultivated and picked cotton until he died of exhaustion two years ago, caught flak and shrapnel in one side on the day after he went back to secure his position. The calf of one leg was smashed to smithereens. The hand and lower part of his left arm disappeared in the explosion.

"All I know is that an old woman with a craggy, crinkled face and no expression in her eyes at all came toward me on the street.

"I shouted for her to halt.

"She kept walking toward me slowly, taking small little steps beneath her dirty pajama-clothes. She just kept looking at me and walking.

"I hollered at her again.

"She was about 20 feet or so away when a friend of mine across the street raised up with his rifle set.

"He shouted and she glanced over in his direction.

"I had my rifle fixed too by this time.

"She pulled her hand out of a pocket in her pants and I saw she had something.

14

"She had her hand drawn back when I pulled the trigger. But it wasn't soon enough. I unloaded, but somehow the grenade fell forward toward me, and before I could get away it exploded."

Later that day, after physicians took care of him at the emergency field hospital, Morrison and other casualties were evacuated amidst gunfire from the Saigon area. They were helped to boats, crossed the river and were transported to awaiting hospitals in a more peaceful zone.

"In the weeks that followed we did a lot of talking on the wards. All of us were hurting—and not just from the wounds. We were bitter that the Army could allow us to be caught in such a vulnerable position.

"All the while we had been in Vietnam we had been thinking we were the winners. The fact that we had a larger body-count than the other side had been drummed into our heads over and over again. The officers had proclaimed every little skirmish in the Delta a tremendous victory for our side. We had not stopped to think if they were real victories—or why they were victories—at that time we didn't have the time, and we didn't feel the necessity. We had killed the VC. We had cleaned up an area, we had thought.

"Obviously, when we were caught with our pants down in Saigon and everywhere else in the country, obviously we weren't winning. We talked about it for hours every day. I think that the morale was never lower. To us, our entire objective for living as a soldier had been defeated. Why had we fought and killed? Why had our buddies dropped at our sides, in front of our eyes, while we had heard their cries? There had been a reason for most of us.

"I went into the service to find myself. I had made decent grades in school. My daddy, who farmed until his hands were solid callous and his brain was baked, liked to read the Bible and Bible stories. He wanted me to be a preacher and be smart. But I didn't see much hope for that. I didn't want to fight a white man's battle in segregated schools while I had to earn his sniveling wages to pay my tuition. And I didn't give one shit about getting myself slaughtered in a battle over civil rights which I thought I deserved without having to fight. So I went into the Army because there I was equal. I had talked to cousins who had made it a career. They had nothing but good things to say. I believed, and I went.

"While I was laying up there in those wards, I wondered why—just like all the others, black and white. We were mad and disgusted, disabled and tired and generally fucked up."

The day of our interview Leon Morrison sat crosslegged at a desk in his small groundfloor apart-

16

ment in an integrated complex on the outskirts of Macon. If you didn't know the bottom part of his left leg was missing, you couldn't tell it. The left hand is a stub with a mechanical fixture on the end. He is able to hold items in the chrome hook with two prongs.

"But you know it wasn't long before the morale started to pick up in the wards—both in Vietnam and in Hawaii. Word came back to us—it's weird how the grapevine works in the service, it's quick and correct, moreso than most newspapers, especially *Stars and Stripes*,—but word came to us that Charley was being overrun in the northern provinces.

"The sonsofbitches who got us are now getting it themselves, we thought. We got reports from some of the wounded who drifted down. We got word from some of our buddies who were still out there fighting. They would come to see us or write or send messages by others.

"Our soldiers were wiping out known Vietcong strongholds from one end of the country to the other. Screw the Souths. If we were going to win the war we had to get rid of the enemy who came out of nowhere. There's no way to tell them by their uniform or the color of their skin or their age or their sex. Hell, man, all the sonsofbitches look alike.

"It wasn't just My Lai. Hell, I'd never heard of My Lai until Lt. Calley was charged. Shit, there were little places in the northern hills. There were villages where Charley kept his women and left his children. More spies came out of those places than anywhere else—and they killed.

"They claimed to be innocent. Sweet and innocent. Shit! As innocent as Hitler! As innocent as the bastards who shoveled Jews into the ovens.

"All up in the area of Quang Ngai, Da Nang, Hue, Quang Tri and Dak To. The South China Sea's coastline was filled with little hamlets where Cong sympathizers reigned. But the American Army went in there and wiped them out. They had to do it. If for no other reason, to save face and to bring the morale of our troops back up to some kind of decent standard.

"Sure, they got a lot of South Vietnamese civilians in the whole business. But isn't it worth it?"

He asked the question with a positive tone, completely void of sarcasm.

Leon Morrison still does not know what he wants to do or what he will be able to do when he graduates. Now he is studying secondary education, but he is dissatisfied with the subjects. He says the courses are dull and insufficient. He also says that the Georgia public school system "has too much of Lester Maddox in it to suit me."

He has been thinking about political science at one of the larger state universities, but he knows that will take more work and a more involved intelligence. He is not sure, he says, that he is willing to put "that much" into his education "at this time."

While his future is up for grabs, he continues to wonder about a yesterday when he made the mistake of not shooting an old lady who held his future in her hand.

Lt. William L. Calley Jr. was not too slow on the draw. His was a different day. He came after the first maneuver of Tet. He arrived in the aftermath of the ten days of hell. But he saw it from a short distance away. He felt its blows.

Having arrived in Vietnam in December of 1967, the company he was assigned to, C Company of the First Battalion in the 20th Infantry, he was sent to conduct patrol missions in the hills of northern South Vietnam.

From there he listened while Ho carried out the threat of Mao Tse-tung, who said, "To put it bluntly, it is necessary to bring about a brief reign of terror in every rural area; otherwise one could never suppress the activities of the counter-revolutionaries."

While the company was nestled in the hills near Dak To in Quang Ngai province about 100 miles west of the village of My Lai Four, a young troop from San Antonio, Texas, along with Calley and others became initiated to the battlefield.

In his own tough way, Eusebio B. Santellana remembers one night in January, approximately two months before the assault on My Lai.

"A patrol had gone out that day. They went up a hill picked out by (Capt. Ernest) Medina. It was known as a VC-held hill. A danger area.

"By night they hadn't come back. Nobody in the whole Goddam platoon ate anything that night. I don't think anybody among us did. We didn't do much talking either. We hadn't had a loss. The hills were as quiet as a Texas desert.

"Sometime in the late night we heard screaming. It was the vomit cry. Like death. But it didn't stop. Not after one time. It kept going. It got weaker and weaker, but it held out. And it'd make you want to shit right there in your tracks. The bastards!

"Nobody slept a wink. Who could? Some of the young guys were crying. You could hear 'em trying to hold back, but they couldn't help it. Goddam, they might be next. What the hell was happening? It made you sicker and sicker.

"The next morning we couldn't help but see what had been going on. The first patrol out ran up on a man's skinned body stuck on a pole.

"Dink shitheads had skinned him alive. We

20

never did find the others. God knows what the son-sofbitches did to them. It makes you want to kill all of them. The way they look at you, cold and hard. And you don't know who's who. They're all a bunch of shits. Sorry as hell. It makes you want to puke your guts out.

"After you live through a little of it, it makes you want to kill all of them. It stinks from way down deep.

"I can't help it, that's the way I am now. And whatever Calley did. . . ."

Santellana was not at My Lai. He was sent back to Texas when a member of his family died, and he did not return.

"Whatever Calley did, it was justified. Nobody should be found guilty for doing what's natural and right. He did it for his country and his fellow man. Goddam, you had to kill."

The first time I saw First Lt. William Laws Calley Jr. I thought it was a frightened look that covered his face.

I could not have been more mistaken.

What was there was a cocky sense of pride which had become as deeply ingrained into his soul as the Star Spangled Banner has into the history of the United States.

The Making of a Hero

His eyes are large and dark, nervous eyes like those of a small calf in an Alabama barnyard. I have seen many such calves. They appear frightened. But it is not fright, it's security which makes them strut so boldly by their mother's side. They have the assurance that whatsoever will happen, the mother will be nearby, will protect and will in the end prevail over any outside forces of evil.

It is this innate security which makes Calley tick. It is an unconscious feeling—not self-assurance—that makes him know that when the little man is stomped on by the giant the populous will rise up in his defense. That's the way of this country.

When he stood in front of the court-martial in that tiny unassuming room in the nondescript red brick building under the shade of the oaks on the grounds of Ft. Benning, Georgia, within a stone's throw of a field where Gen. George S. Patton trained troops for World War Two 30 years before, the five-foot-three-inch lieutenant spoke without blinking an eye.

An emotional nervousness made him trip over two words. But he was not afraid. He spoke out so that all might hear.

"By the guilty verdict," he said, "you stripped me of all honor. Please, by your actions that you take here today (sentencing), don't strip future soldiers of their honor. I beg of you.

"I'm not going to stand here and plead for my life or my freedom.

"I would ask you to consider the thousands more lives that are going to be lost in Southeast Asia. The thousands more, that is, to be imprisoned not only here in the United States, but also in North Vietnam and in hospitals all over the world as amputees.

"I've never known a soldier, nor did I ever myself wantonly kill a human being in my entire life.

"If I've committed a crime, the only crime I have committed is in my judgment of my values. Apparently I have valued my troops' lives more than I did that of my enemy.

"When my troops were getting massacred and mauled by an enemy I couldn't see, I couldn't feel and I couldn't touch; that nobody in the military system ever described as anything other than communism—they didn't give it a race, they didn't give it any sex, they didn't give it an age. They never let me know it was just a philosophy in a man's mind. That was my enemy out there.

"And when it became between me and my enemy, I had to value the lives of my troops. I feel that is the only crime I have committed."

The following day the six officers sitting on the court-martial jury sentenced the young man to life imprisonment.

23

Calley had spoken for a generation of fighting men who had gone to a country they had never even studied in the geography classes of their high school years.

He said the words as a hero should speak them, overflowing with the drama of the moment, honestly and forthrightly. Nevertheless, he was sentenced.

That sentencing echoed across the world, and a cry of disenchantment was returned by the people of his country.

He had been found guilty of killing 22 civilians of South Vietnam, the country the United States had been defending for a decade.

The jury of his peers believed that the evidence was weighed against him.

But the people of the United States didn't believe this. Never would they believe it. The mamas and papas could not believe their sons could do such wrong. The politicians who had shouted war cries in the past were hurt because a soldier had fallen. And the voters who had filled the ballot boxes and had tapped Richard Nixon as the president of their choice in 1968 were suddenly disillusioned because the war was continuing. And the youth who had marched against the shooting in Southeast Asia saw Calley as another victim and another symbol of what was wrong with all wars.

The people shouted and democracy prevailed.

Two days after the sentencing the President freed Calley to be confined in his bachelor apartment on Ft. Benning, where he had been stationed since returning from Vietnam almost two years before.

He did not have to go to prison. At least not at the moment. And he will probably never have to go. Democracy is that way. When it stands on its own two feet and shakes its fist, it gains the upper hand and holds its own.

Now he is in limbo: not allowed into the heaven of ordinary existence but not sentenced to the fires of hell.

Chapter Two

Search

When I first heard the word "massacre," I thought of General Custer and the last stand. My God, that word belongs in a Victorian dictionary. Certainly it doesn't involve life in Twentieth Century America.

But again my first impression was wrong.

In the middle of September in 1969, I received word third-handed from a small group of rebels within the Pentagon that the Army was holding a lieutenant for single-handedly killing a number of South Vietnamese civilians.

I had worked for newspapers half my life. Beginning as a sports reporter when I was in high school in Tuscaloosa, Alabama, I did a column for a weekly and wrote feature stories for the school paper when I attended the University of Alabama.

In 1969, at the age of 29, I had been an investigative reporter for the *Alabama Journal* in Montgomery for four years. I had won several journalism awards during this time, including a special citation from the Associated Press Managing Editors Association. Most importantly, however, the stories published in the *Journal* in association with our sister paper, *The Advertiser*, had managed to uncover many controversial situations of both statewide and national significance. Our editor and publisher, Harold Martin, won a Pulitzer Prize for reporting and continues to encourage in-depth investigation in lieu of the hit-and-miss accounts of sub-standard journalism.

With this background and knowing that if I did come up with enough substantiated details I would be supported, I struck out on the least traveled trail.

Several telephone calls to Ft. Benning, Georgia, the Army post some 90 miles east of Montgomery, where I understood the lieutenant was stationed, brought negative replies from personnel.

Is a soldier being charged?

With murder?

Of South Vietnamese?

Is he an officer?

Simple, basic questions were being asked. No one seemed to know the answers.

But word came back again from the Pentagon that the lieutenant was being held past his release date from the Army.

From past experiences with "reliable" Pentagon sources, I knew the facts would be correct before the "leak" filtered as far away as Montgomery.

A small band of high-grade officers in the Pentagon have been opposed to Vietnam involvement since the beginning. These men have kept the press alert to many facts which would have otherwise been buried in heaps of red tape and official documents. Luckily for the media and for the American public, these rebels want to keep the world informed on both sides of the military. And it was through their clever "leak" that the germ was first planted.

I had no specific official to turn to in Washington. I tried several offices by phone, but each time there were either answers of "No, I'm sure that's not true. If it were true, certainly I would know," or vague words of "Not that I know of, but on another level. . . ."

In Ft. Benning I found likewise answers, when I obtained answers at all.

At the post's judge advocate general's office I discovered no one of status at home.

"When will he return?"

The clerk was not sure. Maybe two days, maybe a week. But most definitely, no one else could talk to a reporter or give out facts about any pending case.

At the post's commanding general's office I was told similar answers. Major General Orwin C. Talbott might return in days, or perhaps a week. And no one present could give any answers pertaining to an officer who might possibly be court-martialed.

It was a ditto situation at the information office. I was told Colonel Douglas B. Tucker, the officer in charge, was not in and not expected that day.

My brain numbed from the negative replies, I started home. Even at an Italian restaurant on the boulevard, Victory Drive, leading from Columbus to the post I was told they were out of ravioli. By this time I was sure there was a conspiracy not only to keep the facts of the case intact but against me personally. Hell, it was a big joke.

All the way home to Montgomery I tried to think of ways to go about breaking the barrier obviously constructed by the vast Army bureaucracy.

From the *Journal* office that night I telephoned a

half-dozen friends: politicians, attorneys and a writer.

The writer was Alabama novelist and reporter William Bradford Huie, a man in whom I have a great deal of respect and whose work has been studied and admired by a countless number of young reporters.

Huie, who had broken down a similar blockade of pious hiding of facts in his investigation into the case of the only deserter hanged during World War Two, listened sympathetically.

I had read Huie's "The Execution of Private Slovik," which tells detail by detail of the crime, court-martial and death of Ernie Slovik. It is one of the finest pieces of reporting ever published, and I knew that his advice would be invaluable.

Less than three months before we had had a long lunch together at his home in Hartselle, Alabama, and he had discussed some of the investigative work he had done on his book, "He Slew The Dreamer," an expose into the circumstances surrounding the assassination of Dr. Martin Luther King Jr. by James Earl Ray. Huie's book tells the story of Ray before and after the killing, and it too is a superb job of laying the facts bare.

When I finished, Huie said, "Who is the highest

ranked politician you know in Washington?"

I thought for a moment. I knew Alabama's senators, John Sparkman and Jim Allen, only slightly. But I did know them.

"See if you can get them to work for you on that end. And what about your congressman?"

Sure, I thought; why hadn't I thought of Rep. William L. Dickinson? I had known Bill Dickinson through two campaigns, including the first when he ran as a Republican and defeated the Democratic incumbent in the Barry Goldwater Southern sweep of 1964. He remained one of Alabama's only three Republican congressmen to hold their own.

Dickinson, a tall, handsome, amiable fellow who looks more like a fullback for the Atlanta Falcons than a grass roots politician, worked hard in his years in Congress and has been placed on several important committees, including the Armed Service Committee. I was positive he would be able to help —at least to some degree.

The first priority on my schedule the next morning was a call to Dickinson's Washington office. An aide said the congressman was out of town but would be back that evening.

I described what I knew about the Army situation and emphasized that I was positive there was much more to the situation than any authority wanted to release. I also told him there was a cover-up of the facts by the Army and that even someone in Dickinson's position might have considerable difficulty obtaining the truth.

The following day Dickinson returned my call. He said he had been briefed on my conversation, and I reiterated what I suspected.

Within the week Dickinson got in touch with me again and repeated a conversation he had had with an officer at the Pentagon.

The officer confirmed the fact that a lieutenant was being held for an investigation at Ft. Benning on "misdoings" in South Vietnam. Little else came out of the conversation, but Dickinson said he would continue to probe into the situation.

Armed only with these bare facts, I confronted my editor with the possibility of my returning to Ft. Benning—this time for a full week of looking into the situation.

Ours is a small daily with a circulation of approximately 30,000 and a staff of eight reporters. And at that time we had only six reporters. For one to be away for a week might cause a hardship on everyday production.

However, I had the backing of my city editor, Joe McFadden, and Harold Martin heard me out.

"This seems like the largest story of the war yet," I argued. "If it's true it could be another Nuremberg and inevitably it might end the war."

"Atrocities, if you want to call them that, happened every day of World War Two," said Martin.

"But none have really been reported from this war," I said.

And with that Martin agreed to let me go to Ft. Benning but to return if I found the situation hopeless. He also said he knew of no strings he could pull in Washington to get the story from that end.

Ft. Benning, as it had been before, was a pleasant place with huge pine trees and a constant cool breeze during the autumn. But it was a place where officers in the highest positions of authority had suddenly disappeared during the first week of November of 1969.

Again I started at the top. Again I found Talbott, Tucker and others away from their offices. And I was told all were off the post.

However, during my second day, on the way across a flat shaded green field, after talking to a blockade sergeant, I saw a man walking briskly down the sidewalk. On his breast was enough brass to sink a small yacht. And I recognized his face from a photograph I had seen in an office on the post.

As I approached, I smiled and nodded. "General?" I said.

He responded, and I introduced myself and stepped with him.

When I asked my questions he said I would have to see Col. Tucker about details concerning the lieutenant in question.

With that, curtly but politely, Talbott stepped into a waiting car and was driven away.

The Public Information Office people assured me again that Col. Tucker was out.

For the first time I knew everything that I suspected was right. There was a cover-up—and there was something here bigger than I had imagined.

That afternoon I begged my city editor to let me remain in Georgia for another day although I was empty-handed thus far. Reluctantly, he agreed.

I spent that evening questioning waitresses in local bistros and bartenders at clubs on Victory Drive. Nobody knew anything.

The next morning I was waiting in the information office when Col. Tucker arrived.

I overheard a clerk greet him and as I neared I read his name tag.

Before he entered his inner-office, I stepped up and offered my hand. I quickly introduced myself and said I had been waiting to see him for two days.

Inside his office, I told Tucker that I had confronted Gen. Talbott with my questions.

"I've come to you for the answers," I said.

Tucker explained that other reporters from much

larger papers had been seeking similar information. He said, however, that the information could not yet be released—only that a lieutenant was being investigated.

I asked more questions.

None of them were answered.

On my way back to Montgomery that afternoon I searched my mind for some possible clue, some source, some speck of information which I might have overlooked; but nothing came to mind.

Back at the office, after explaining that I had failed, I began calling all sources again.

From one Washington office I obtained the name of an officer at the Pentagon who might help. The aide of Rep. Dickinson said this man had "seemed cooperative."

I telephoned. I told the official about the run-around I had been getting, but that I was sure other information must be available.

He said simply, "Try for the files of First Lt. William L. Calley. He should have been released from the Army 6 September this year. I believe you will find he is being held over. That's all I can tell you."

I pressed him on what, how and why. By this time I was excited with the possibilities of disclosure. Only a beginning had been made, but some instinct said there had to be something else from this man.

Finally, after repeating that he knew nothing else, he gave me the name of another man at the Pentagon and the extension.

Minutes later, another officer told me the same facts.

When more questions came, he said, "He's being investigated for the murder of 91 persons."

"Ninety-one?"

"I'm almost positive that's the figure."

"Are you positive?"

"I'd say 91, or more—an entire village in South Vietnam."

"What village?"

"I'm not sure of the name."

"When did this Lt. Calley allegedly kill these people?"

"More than a year ago. In March, 1968."

"An entire village?"

"Men, women and children."

"Children?"

"That's right."

More questions failed to bring answers. I thanked the colonel.

That evening I spent three hours convincing my city editor that I had enough facts for a story and persuading him that it was the big story.

Again I called William Bradford Huie. I told him what I had and said, "Would you go with that?"

He said that in his newspaper days he would write it as quickly as possible and print it and copyright it—although we had little more than "audacity" going for us.

The next morning I started to write my story. But one last time I called the information office at Ft. Benning.

This time I got Tucker who said he had been authorized to release "preliminary details." I began questioning.

The following by-lined but not copyrighted story appeared below a banner headline in the City Edition of the *Alabama Journal* on November 12, 1969:

A 26-year-old Army officer at Ft. Benning, Ga., is being investigated on charges of "the multiple murder of civilians of South Vietnam."

Informed sources told the *Journal* the officer is suspected of wiping out an entire South Vietnamese village by killing 91 people—men, women and children.

Lt. William L. Calley, an infantry officer, "has been told that allegations have been made against him," the public information officer at Ft. Benning said.

Col. Douglas B. Tucker said, however, that Calley was not under arrest and is not being confined to barracks.

After an Article 32 investigation under the military code was made, Tucker said, "it took a stenographer about two weeks to transcribe the report."

The case, originally ordered by Calley's brigade commander, has not been referred to the commanding officer at Ft. Benning, Maj. Gen. Orwin C. Talbott.

"In complicated cases like this one, it may take a couple of weeks before the general gets the case," Tucker commented.

Calley, who lists his home town as Waynesville, N.C., joined the Army in July 1966 in Albuquerque, N.M. He was born in Miami.

The alleged slayings took place in March 1968, little more than a year after Calley arrived in South Vietnam. (He actually arrived in Vietnam in December of 1967.)

The information officer at Ft. Benning told the *Journal* the office there got the case for investigation at the end of August this year.

If the case comes to trial it will be at Ft. Benning, Tucker said.

Under the military code, an Article 32 investigation is similar to a civilian grand jury. The investigation results in a recommendation to the appropriate authority as to whether there should be a court-martial. Then authorities have to approve a trial, if one is to be held.

If the commanding general approves this trial, the information officer said, the case then goes to the judge advocate general, who will prepare the prosecution.

Defending Calley is civilian attorney George Latimer of Salt Lake City, Utah. Latimer is a retired judge on the Military Court of Appeals.

The following morning the *Washington Post* and *The New York Times* had accounts of Calley being held.

The *Post* was among 30 newspapers carrying Seymore M. Hersh's story from Dispatch News Service.

Almost all other papers in the country carried a one-paragraph story from Associated Press out of Atlanta which read: "Army officials say they have completed an investigation into charges of multiple murder of Vietnamese civilians by a young American lieutenant, but that a decision whether to try him remains to be made."

The next day when I called Pentagon information officers, no one would comment.

Then I went to the official with whom I had talked two days before. I read the story as it had appeared. He said that it corresponded with the facts in the *Post*, but the number of persons killed was apparently 109. During hearings this figure was later lowered to 102.

I asked if he could make any comment, adding that again I would not use his name.

"It's obvious that certain officials within the U.S. Army have attempted to hide the facts behind one of the most hideous crimes in its history.

"It has been substantiated that the Army has a defendant under investigation for what might be termed a massacre.

"The obvious hypocrisy demonstrated by some of the highest officials in the military is indefensible. In this case it borders on crime itself."

He added that he had been wanting someone to ask him to comment, and after his retirement gave much more assistance.

Within the next week more and more of the facts about Calley and My Lai Four came to the surface. Not only newspapers but television and the news magazines caught fire with the story. Almost every reporter in every media was trying to develop more facts behind what was happening and what had happened.

Leading the pack was Seymore Hersh. He caught more national headlines and spotlights and uncovered more of the uncoverable during those first weeks. He worked hard and made the biggest splash, especially with his exceptional interview with Paul Meadlo and other follow-up stories— and for his work he won a well-deserved special Pulitzer Prize.

Chapter Three

Book

You never know from one day to the next what will happen when you're playing the newspaper game. That's what makes it so vitally interesting, and it's impossible to sit on the bench and watch others do the work.

As always, those November days passed quickly. So much happened. Dozens of phone calls were made. Hundreds of miles were driven.

Ft. Benning, that place of a million giant

Southern pines, perfectly groomed grass-carpeted islands between wide boulevards, neat little insignificant buildings lined up like a toy town, became my home during those days.

A huge reservation with a population of more than 60,000, troops have come and gone; they arrived innocent of death; they leave knowing exactly how to kill. Either with their bare hands in a karate punch that would sever the heart within a yellow body or penetrate a stack of a quartet of brick . . . or with the M16, a dynamite of a rifle, modernistically and economically and humanistically, designed to kill and not to maim.

On a knoll in the northern section of the huge war plant is a neat log "cabin" with a well-lighted parking lot and manicured grounds. This is the Sand Hill Officers Club. Donated to the fighting man by Gen. George S. Patton, it was his home prior to World War Two. He and his wife lived in the eight-room affair. In the valleys he trained his men for the next war. On the fields he ran his polo ponies as any gentleman soldier should do when he's not fighting a battle. And once Old Blood and Guts took two of his tanks to the river bridge in downtown Columbus and pointed his guns toward the infamous Phenix City, Alabama, where two of his trainees were being held in jail without bond for beating up a bartender, or so the story goes. Needless to say, the authorities released the lads to their leader before the guns were actually used, according to local folklore connoisseurs.

Whether it's true is really not important. It's like the tales of West Point, the lies, the tall ones which are elaborated on each year by a new cadet class. At Ft. Benning, of course, it's a redneck version of the sophisticated military academy on the banks of the Hudson. But it does have its traditions. It does have its own brand of spirit.

Twenty-four-year-old Sgt. William L. Calley arrived at Ft. Benning in 1967 and began his training to become an officer in the U.S. Army. He walked beneath the same great trees under which I strode the day after the first story appeared in the *Journal.*

Col. Tucker had arranged for three reporters to meet and ask Calley a few questions. I was included in the trio.

When we were taken to a room in the white frame typical PIO building, we were confronted with a wide-eyed youth with receding auburn hair.

Flashing a winning smile, he stood and shook hands with us.

Five-feet-three-inches. One-hundred-thirty-pounds. Bronze Star with Oak Leaf Cluster was clasped to the breast of his ultra neat uniform. Also a Purple Heart.

Elbows leaning on the bare table, he crushed out

one Marlboro and lighted another.

"Reporters have been telephoning me constantly. I'm having my number changed. It'll be unlisted."

He has a nervous twitch in his right jaw when he speaks. And his eyes are watery and jittery.

Asked if he had been confined, he said, "Last week I was in Miami to visit my dad. I hope my family is left out of this. They don't know anything."

He was born and raised in Miami. Originally he had listed his home town as Waynesville, N.C., but he said that was because he spent part of one summer there. It was sort of camouflage.

He spent one year at Palm Beach Junior College in Lake Worth, Florida, where he said he was an "average student." Later I discovered he left school after making four F's during his first year. He explained it then: "I took a general education course and was okay, I guess, but it just seemed like the 13th year in high school."

In 1964, after he left college, he worked as a strike-breaker pick-up worker on the Florida East Coast Railway. His only jail record on the books anywhere, he said, was when he allowed a train to block an intersection too long during his railroad stint.

As an appraiser for an insurance company, he worked his way west from New Orleans to New

Mexico. "It didn't take much skill. I just took pictures of buildings and let someone else figure out how much they were worth."

By this time the 1-Y draft deferment he had as a railroad workman had lapsed and he became afraid he would be drafted soon. In Albuquerque he enlisted in 1966. After attending officers' school at Ft. Benning in 1967, he was shipped to Vietnam in December of that year.

Asked why he volunteered for additional duty in the Southeast Asian country after his normal one-year tour had elapsed, he said he believed in his nation's military role in Vietnam. "I guess everyone has their own feelings about the war. I doubt I can explain all of mine.

"I had planned to stay in the Army for at least a few more years, until this happened. I wasn't sure whether to make it a career or not."

Bombs drop on the southern part of the 150,000-plus acres which has become the Vietnamese training ground for troops going to that country. The resounding echoes shake the earth at times. Not tremendously. No, with a subtlety which reminds you that there is a war somewhere over yonder.

In that sector miles south of where we were interviewing that Thursday afternoon there are dozens of tiny mock Vietnamese villages built by the U.S. Corp of Engineers as exact replicas of the real thing. It was in this area and across the Chatahoochee River into Alabama—also Ft. Benning land—that was used as a setting for John Wayne to whip up on the VC in his Batjac Production of "Green Berets."

In November of 1969 it was the job of Lt. Amory S. Anderson to teach young men how to kill. "We regard that simple task as the order of the day," the 28-year-old balding officer from El Paso, Texas, said.

With winter approaching he was as brown as a beachcomber. His eyes were narrowed naturally into a constant squint. His thin lips rapped out the words in military fashion, not hesitating for sideline comments.

We rode in a jeep into the jungle-like area, where mortar boxes, villages and the whole works were set up for the next group of trainees. "This is not unlike the My Lai situation, as I understand it," he pointed out, also explaining that the river, about two miles to the east of us, would be the South China Sea in Vietnam. But even at that you would have to switch directions. Somehow the directions didn't matter at that moment.

I was noticing the thatch-roofed huts, the white stucco cottages sans doors, the deep-rutted dirt passageways between the houses. There were about three dozen cottages and a half-dozen huts, or hooches, as the soldiers call them.

"Several hundred people could live in a hamlet this size. Especially if there are others in the area—which is usually the case.

"We always have accurate intelligence reports as to the physical layout of the target."

Even at Pinkville?

"Certainly there. Charlie Company had been in there twice before that final assault when Calley and his platoon went in. They had been knocked every way but right by the time those boys entered the place. Of course, it was all spread out over a period of about a month—but that's the report we get.

"What happened originally, I don't know. When the first company went in, about a month before Calley and his group, they got knocked to smithereens. Why? That's the question you ask after many skirmishes. The Cong is smart as hell. That's something so many folks don't realize back here at home. They're smart. Maybe smarter than we are. Sure as hell they were during those first two assaults on Pinkville and the My Lai villages. And sure as hell they were during Tet. Damn, man, they caught us standing still doing nothing, flatfooted.

"You can believe that the first platoon knew

49

where everything was when they went in. We've got excellent maps. Intelligence knows its business on that score, even in Vietnam.

"But the people are something else again. You have to count heads? It's impossible. My God, they've got more mobility. And you see, it's their country. They know where and when to move. They know how to move. Right there at Pinkville you should have seen the tunnel network through the bunkers and under the village. It's miraculous, the native engineering strength of those people.

"We tend to sit back and underestimate them. I mean, after all, since we've been fighting that sonofabitch of a war we've gone to the moon. You've been able to sit in your living room and watch men crawling around up there on the moon. Damn, can you imagine the know-how, the strength, the capability and everything else that that takes?

"But we can't go in and take a simple little country filled with empty-headed gooks. It should piss folks off, but I don't reckon it ever will.

"You start asking yourself those questions and it'll put you to thinking. You look out over a little layout like this one, just to get a feel of the place without the people, and it doesn't mean a whole lot. Look at it, the little ole houses and shacks; looks easy, doesn't it?

"Then you put some smart little people in there who know where everything is and who are afraid of you because you've come to kill. They're hard to get to.

"We've asked ourselves a lot of questions about why they're so tough. I don't know. But you know, maybe it's plain ole survival."

Two weeks after the Calley story broke, after several other participants of the My Lai affair had been charged with crimes by the Army, I took an afternoon off from the newspaper grind.

One of my best friends, George W. Dean from Destin, Florida, had two marijuana cases he was trying that afternoon in Opelika, about 50 miles east of Montgomery.

One of that rare breed of Southerner, a maverick liberal attorney, Dean is a tall prematurely gray lover of conversation and constant controversy. He was driving that sunny afternoon as we started toward the Lee County Courthouse where his clients, Auburn University students, waited for his appearance.

We were not out of the Montgomery city limits before he began questioning me about the Calley case. He had talked about it previously in excited tones, giving his idea that it was the biggest legal happening in military history since Nazi leaders were tried and sentenced and executed after World War Two. He had originally convinced me of the importance via long distance telephone from his home in Destin, and during frequent visits to Montgomery, where he was born and raised.

"What kind of person is he?" Dean asked about Calley.

I repeated that I immediately liked the little man, that I found him to be interesting although not particularly bright and that he could be termed an average American boy caught up in a terrible tragedy. It was a tragedy, I felt, not of his own making but a product of the Army and its oftentimes ridiculous system. "If he killed all those people, the sonofabitch should be hung," I said.

"Do you really feel that way?"

"Certainly I do, especially since the victims were little children and women. That's an unthinkable crime."

"What about dropping a bomb on Hiroshima?"

"That's horrible, but it's not looking each victim in the face and pulling the trigger. It's not that cold blooded. It's not that personal."

"But it is killing women and children and old people. I grant that it's not the same, but it is as deadly." Dean continued, outlining my news stories and others which had appeared: Paul Meadlo's emotional confession on nationwide television describing the killings, Ron Haeberle's frightening photographs of the results of the massacre published in *Life, Time* and *Newsweek* cover stories, the military's panel appointed to study earlier Army investigations into the My Lai Four incident and other publicity of the past two weeks.

"Have you ever seen anything take the nation—hell, the world—so completely into its grasp?"

I was looking out the window, thinking about everything I had heard, had read, had seen and felt during the time since the story first broke.

The world was torn apart by the assassination of President Kennedy. People wept on the streets. But this is altogether different. This involves a whole decade of torture, fighting, boys-next-door being killed in a Goddamn place so far away nobody had heard of it until the first shot was fired. It involves an entire generation of young people: those who fought and lived, those who fought and died, and those who stayed home and fought the war by protesting in their own ways.

"Calley is a catharsis of the Vietnam War. It's the biggest story of the decade, I'm convinced of that," he said.

We continued talking, bantering back and forth ideas about the man and the situation.

"You were the first one there. You should write

the book. It is a book. Hell, maybe two books," Dean said.

Again our talk became dialogue. Both of us were so enthralled in our words and thoughts that before we knew it we were 25 miles beyond the cutoff to our destination. Dean looked up and said, "Damn! You know where we are?"

Surprised, I shrugged.

"Georgia!"

"Jesus!"

More than a year later, while we were sitting in his shaded Florida lawn looking out over the Choctawhatchee Bay, Dean said, "You know what we were doing that day? We were on a Freudian trip. We were heading for Ft. Benning and didn't even know it."

As soon as we turned around and got back to Opelika I telephoned George Latimer, Calley's attorney in Salt Lake City, from the county clerk's office.

I found the elderly gentleman at his office and he quickly replied to my query: "I'm sure my client would most definitely be interested in a book.

"I'm sure he would be interested in talking to you."

He said that he had preliminary motions to file within the next week, and asked if I would call him back in ten days.

That evening I sent a telegram of confirmation and the next morning a letter.

Chapter Four

Lieutenant

Again Calley was in full dress. He was not as obviously nervous as he had been a month earlier, but he still chainsmoked and this time he wanted a drink.

We were in Latimer's small apartment on the post, meeting for the first time in the casual atmosphere of talk and drink. Earlier that day five of the charges had been dropped; he was now charged with 102 deaths.

The boyish face seemed even more out of place now as he mixed a round of bourbon for all but the attorney. In fact, he appeared not unlike the miniature soldiers playing Army many years ago on the empty lot in Birmingham.

He was not at all ill-at-ease during that first time we sat together and discussed doing a book. He appeared more worried about money than anything else, but he also wanted to talk—about Vietnam, the war, the people he had known, the girls he had been with and himself.

During the next two months we spent much time together. I went to Benning to his small bachelor's apartment in the shingle-covered two-story building near the main officer's club. We met in downtown Columbus where I had a room at a motel some weekends. We went to Atlanta together once. And several times he traveled to Montgomery and spent weekends.

About a week after our first meeting I went to see him at his place. We talked about Vietnam and his situation after he came back from the war. Afterwards we went to the officer's club and began to drink.

While we drank we talked about his life and this country and where we're going and what we're going to do when we get there.

Lifting his glass and tilting his head to one side,

he liked to spout platitudes by the dozens. He enjoyed taking stands, even if it meant changing his mind a few minutes or an hour later.

"There are no heroes in Vietnam," he said in the relaxed conversation. "There never are any heroes until you've won or you're winning."

"I'm no hero," he added a few minutes later, after the chatter of the bar became louder around us, after another round was served.

"I wasn't a hero, I lost half my men," he said. "It was terrible, and nothing can make that right.

"As long as we have one guy in Vietnam, I'll keep fighting this thing (court-martial). I love the Army. I'm not just fighting this for myself. I'm fighting for every guy over there, and for every one who has died over there."

Throughout our friendship, his love for the Army was his undying devotion. He never went against the institution which had taken him in and which had mothered him. After all, it was his family. When he got into trouble, it would punish him and it would also look after him and guard him from the evils of the world.

"I'm for the Army all the way," he said on one of our trips. "I'm behind it, a member of it. As long as I'm sitting here with a uniform on, the Army comes first."

I had been arguing that the military was making a

scapegoat of him. I said that he should expose the bastards for what they really were. At that time I did not realize the depth of his devotion.

"Every country needs an Army," he added. "I don't believe in every move Judge Latimer makes for my defense. And I won't, no matter how much Judge Latimer tells me I should to help my own defense, I won't make any statements derogatory about the Army.

"When the Army of a country is defeated, it no longer has law and order. There is a breakdown when that happens.

"People have written to me—telling me that my defense is beginning this breakdown. One man sent me a book about the proletariat takeover of Russia—about the Czar's army being taken over from the inside. That was the first move the Communists made. But in the United States, if I can help it—and there're plenty more like me—nothing similar to that will ever happen. I believe in the Army. Where we go wrong is in Congress, in the politicians. They make policy in Vietnam, but they don't know what's happening over there. They should give the authority to the Army."

One of his pastimes during this period of his life was flying to Atlanta and sitting in the lounges in the airport.

While he sipped bourbon or beer he'd watch the

airplanes come and go and would speculate on their destinations. "I like to dream about going to all the foreign lands in the world," he said once, watching a huge jet taxi down the runway.

He always liked to go first-class. While on one hand he felt threatened by strangers staring at him, he enjoyed the notoriety. Every afternoon at news time he found a television to see where he was being played. If the networks dropped his case for a day, he'd be disappointed. If the newsmen only gave him a minute, he felt as though it was worth much more. And in the mornings he looked for newspapers to check the headlines.

One evening as we sat in the Delta lounge and watched endless jets land and take off at the Atlanta Airport, he said, "Now this is really enjoying yourself. You know what I mean? It's enjoying the world." And he looked back out the window toward the long expanse of dull concrete and shiny chrome planes.

And another time, as we sat in the antebellum living room of my ancient apartment in Montgomery, he announced out of the blue: "I won't say anything derogatory about anyone. I like people, and I won't say anything against anybody. There's nobody that I dislike. Even to help myself, to help my case, I won't shoot down someone else. I couldn't do that, I won't do it. I'm not made like that. Ever since I can remember, I've learned not to knock down somebody else just to save your own skin."

When we met older friends of mine, he was always extremely polite. The military mannerisms were deep within him. Mother had trained her obedient son well, and with certain maturity the son appreciated the strict up-bringing.

The Army became his family soon after he entered into the service. He even liked boot camp. He enjoyed the tough discipline, something which surprised him; he had never been disciplined before in his entire 23 years.

His father was not a well man. He had not been for more than a half-dozen years.

Calley felt much closer to his mother, a stern woman with a deep and abiding layer of kindness beneath Presbyterian knowledge that whatever will be will be. Had she been alive when he was charged she would have known it was an act of something bigger than any of them, according to friends who knew the family.

But she died shortly after he went into the Army. Two of his sisters were older, but they had families of their own to look after. The other took care of his father. And anyway, he was a military man; he had wars to fight.

He had never made a success of anything that he

tried to accomplish. And he had never tried to accomplish much. He had never brought any mountains into focus and never enjoyed climbing anyway.

As long as the world kept turning, Calley knew he would rotate with it.

"When a soldier has this attitude you never have to worry about his future in the Army," said a training officer at Benning.

"He'll never question an order. He knows instinctively that the man who ranks above him has more knowledge and wisdom of the situation than he does. And there is always somebody who ranks above him.

"I'd say, from what I know of Lt. Calley, that he's a damn good soldier.

"You don't want a half-assed do-gooder or somebody who's always trying to get ahead. They're nothing but trouble.

"You take a little guy who doesn't have a whole hell of a lot of ambition and drive but will follow an order. I'll take him over the smart one every time."

Another pastime was water-skiing. He would take his runabout with its outboard motor to nearby Lake Harding in Alabama where he would often spend weekends at a friend's cabin. Most of the daylight hours would be occupied by running the boat up and down the lake, pulling someone else or being pulled. "I'm no expert at this stuff, but it's fun. You can whip back and forth and try some tricks. It's a great feeling, coasting across the water like you're flying.

"I've thought I'd like to fly, but I never have had time to learn.

"Kind of makes me sick sometimes to think of all the things I've missed, all the things I'd like to do and haven't done.

"I really like to travel. I do. I like to get in a jet with a pilot up front who really knows what he's doing. Makes me feel comfortable.

"I like to visit new and different places. I liked Vietnam. It's beautiful country.

"I went through Europe once, a whirlwind visit, but I liked even that. I guess I could travel all the time and never get tired of it."

His basic ambition was to be a good soldier. More than once he told me he wished the My Lai affair would just go away. "If it'd disappear I'd like to go back to Vietnam or Laos or Cambodia. I loved that country. I loved being a soldier over there. I would hope that the war's over, but I could remain. Sometimes now I dream about that.

"I did a good job for the Army. I was a good soldier. I made some mistakes, but I became a better-than-average officer.

"Smart? Hell, it took 'em a month to teach me how to run up a hill."

"When you first get to know him you don't exactly know how to take him," said one of Calley's former commanders.

"After you get to know him, you leave him alone," the captain said.

"We went into Laos and Cambodia. It was a tough mission behind-the-lines. Those boys had to tough it out the best they could, but they accomplished what we planned to do. And I can't say what that was.

"Calley thought of it as intrigue, I believe. He thought of it as a fantastic game. You see soldiers like that now and then, and when you see it you don't want to change their attitude. It's the best outlook you can have if you're going to be an officer.

"That wasn't to say he wasn't serious. On the contrary, he was as serious as he could be. Like I said, though, it's a serious game with them.

"I could put it this way: I was glad he was on my side.

"Apparently he was clumsy as hell in the Pinkville situation. But when I knew him he was right on target. He loved the jungles and the mountain country.

65

"He changed from any all-American boy image when he got in that green land. It's beautiful back there, and the women you've got working with you are lovely, and he felt it all the way down into his balls.

"I was glad he fought by my side."

Chapter Five

Close-up

When Calley was in high school he was neither a loner nor the most popular in his class.

Today his nickname is Rusty, given to him when he was in the ninth grade by a friend.

If you've seen him on television or on the cover of a news magazine or in the hundreds of newspapers which have carried his photograph, you've seen the young man who still looked like a high school youth when he was charged in 1969.

Lawrence Evans, a classmate with Calley in Miami more than ten years ago, remembers him as a "friendly sort of guy who never got in anybody's way, never caused any trouble and never was anything very special."

Evans, now a real estate agent in Orlando, tells the story, "Once Rusty and another guy, one of his best friends, were out running around in the guy's car drinking beer.

"The guy, I forget his name, pulled up beside me and my date and started giving it some pretty rough language. I didn't appreciate it, and I noticed that Rusty told him to keep it down.

"The guy said 'shit' or something like that and kept on. Rusty took him by the arm and said something else to him; I don't know what. But afterwards the guy didn't say anything else; he just sat there and grinned and looked at us.

"When we got to the next traffic light I pulled alongside them, and the guy didn't say another word. Rusty gave me the high sign. I nodded and mouthed 'thanks,' and we didn't see 'em again that night.

"You know, that guy was bigger than Rusty, and he didn't have to do that. You know, he's a pretty decent fellow."

Another fellow classmate, Bill Johnson, who still lives in Miami, says that he remembers Calley as "a cocky little guy with never anything to say.

"He never jumped into any intellectual conversations over his head. He stayed to himself, dated a few girls I knew. As far as I can remember, he never made a splash with the people who did anything at all—like having parties on the beach or meeting at some teen club or somebody's house.

"His family, although I didn't know them well, were good decent lower middle-class folks. We'd call them straight, honest Americans today. They'd probably be for Nixon, but it's not hard to imagine them supporting George Wallace.

"He had some attractive sisters, all of them sweet pretty girls as I recall. They married nice, decent men and left town.

"You could find thousands of families like that right here in Miami. Wouldn't be difficult at all."

Another friend, Carroll "Buzz" Stone, who now lives in Tampa, remembers, "Rusty was no poor kid. He wasn't rich either.

"I don't remember that he worked anywhere when he went to high school or to Palm Beach College. But he had a car. It wasn't a new Mustang or anything like that. It was a couple of years old. But he wasn't wanting.

"We used to go water-skiing now and then. And

once we went skin-diving down south of The Beach. I don't remember anything significant about it. We liked it, but we didn't try anything too fancy. Nobody was hurt.

"Rusty never did do anything very funny, like show-off for the girls or pull any stunts. He wasn't that type. He was straight down the middle. Just an average sort of fellow who took himself halfway serious and never got into any trouble."

He would never have anything to do with demonstrating for peace or for civil rights.

That's one thing his family is sure of. He was a "good boy." When he wasn't doing anything in particular he'd go down to the local poolhall and watch the other guys shoot billiards. But he was always on the outside edge. He was never in the middle of the action.

He obviously enjoyed the prosperity of the late fifties and early sixties.

Once when he was a teenager he was sent to Georgia Military Academy but returned to graduate from Miami Edison Senior High School in a class of 731.

He became a member of the school's debate squad, and was elected to the Mike and Mask Club.

His best subjects were government and English history, he said.

After leaving Palm Beach Junior College he became a drifter. He worked as a hotel bellhop, dishwasher in a restaurant and became a switchman on the striking railroad.

While he was working on the railroad, finally as a freight-train conductor, his father's business—he sold heavy construction equipment—began to fail and his mother became ill with terminal cancer.

His father sold the stucco house in Miami where Rusty had been raised. The father and mother moved to a cabin in North Carolina.

While on the railroad Calley helped his father financially and attempted to give him moral support as well.

Finally the strike ended and he had to leave the employment of the railroad.

In the same Ford he had had when he was in school, he headed northwest to New Orleans. He had always wanted to go to Mardi Gras and now he was there with empty pockets and no job in sight.

He walked the streets of the festival-singing town and took several temporary jobs until he was finally hired as a photographer for an insurance appraiser, free-lance. This was traveling work, and it took him from Louisiana to New Mexico, where he enlisted in the Army in the middle of the spring.

The oldest of his three sisters, Mrs. Marian Keesling of Gainesville, Florida, told me shortly after he was charged that Rusty was "one of the kindest natured people I've ever known."

She said that he had always been gentle with animals and she could not remember him ever hurting a person.

She said that he had had a few girl friends around Miami "but nothing was ever really serious."

She said that her brother once clothed and fed a little Vietnamese girl. When he returned one evening he found the girl's house bombed, he said. The girl was missing. "He was pretty broken up about the child," she said.

A pretty blonde with whom he had had several dates while he was in high school was named Bonnie Givens. Two years younger than Calley, she said "he was nothing but a very sweet person.

"Rusty was never real out-going. He took everything in stride. He was quiet and sort of shy. Many of the girls in my class thought he was cute. We thought that maybe he didn't date much because he was so short, but I thought it was because he really was shy.

"We used to go out on simple dates—to the movie, once or twice to the beach. He liked to drink a lot of beer and I didn't care for that very much.

"Once I remember we were out at a hot dog and milk shake place. We were parked in his car, waiting for the girl to come and take our order.

"We hadn't said much to each other, just small-talk to pass the time. Finally the waitress came out in a pair of tight shorts and a low-cut top. Her boobs were almost hanging out. She said something to Rusty sort of sexy like and rubbed her boobs up close to his window. And he blushed. He turned a bright pink and when I giggled, after the girl was gone, he blushed again.

"I don't think he took me out but once after that. He must have thought I was making fun of him, or something."

He had two weekend affairs while in Vietnam with an attractive brownette from a small town in North Alabama, who wished to remain anonymous. Now a 25-year-old secretary in Atlanta, Georgia, she was a donut girl in Vietnam for two years.

"That title 'donut girl' is so much bullshit," she said one evening over cocktails in the rooftop lounge of the Regency Hyatt House.

Her hair long and her figure lithe, she had grown accustomed to the sophistications of the Southern capital. "About the only thing that 'donut girl' sig-

nifies to me is that I came to offer the boys a hole,"
she said, without cracking a smile.

"Rusty Calley was one of many sad young boys I
went with while I was over there. I'm not bragging
about how many I had, but it's really not that terrible when you realize the situation.

"Damn, if they didn't have me or other girls like
me they'd be sleeping with filthy Asian whores.
And they are filthy.

"One of the first things I learned was how to
check boys out subtly for VD. If you're fixing to go
to bed with him, give it a little playful twist. You
can look like you're fixing to go down on him, and
all you're doing is checking him out.

"I also learned how to stay clean with douche,
and I was kept supplied with pills.

"My type of girl is probably the best thing going
for the guys over there. They never caught a disease
from girls like me, and we all had a lot of fun. We
girls got to go to the best hotels and see the world
and be fed great food and beautiful drinks. I really
loved it.

"Rusty Calley and I had two very nice weekends
together. From our hotel room we could hear the
bombings of Tet all around.

"He had taken time off from the field. They knew
something big was coming off in their area, but they
didn't know what.

"Rusty said all hell had broken out once before, and a lot of guys had gotten killed in some place called Pinkville.

"When you've got a guy like that, when you're together in the bed and you make love, you realize it might be his last time to be with a woman. You want to be the best woman in the world for him. You want the last love to be his best.

"It's romantic when you hold him and hear his heart beat next to yours. How long will it beat?

"Like I don't care much for making it with anybody any more. I mean, it's the thing you're supposed to do and everything, and everybody does it; but sometimes I think about going back over to Vietnam with something, just so I can hold a guy like that again.

"Damn, it's hell when the bombs are going off all around and you hear people screaming in the streets and the room where you're sleeping starts to shake. You grab for the guy you're with and you hold him as tightly as possible and you try to forget there's a war going on—but you can't forget.

"We had two weekends like that. He was an angel. Like he brought me a present one time. It was real cute.

"But I haven't seen him since, except on television."

She stared out across the top of Atlanta toward

the west as though she thought she could see the blaze of gunfire and the smoke of a bomb in the distance.

The girl with whom he has been going steady throughout the ordeal of his charge, court-martial and sentence is pretty, redheaded Anne Moore.

She is a comely, soft-spoken young lady who has watched all the action from the backseat but who did not let him down for a moment during the tense time.

A retired Army official who had looked extensively into the Calley case told me that he saw no pattern in the background to justify the committing of a mass killing.

"He has what seems like a normal background, varying slightly here and there. But it seems too normal sometimes.

"He might be the victim of a syndrome I saw many times in my 30 years in the U. S. Army.

"Some young men when they enter the service become like robots. They don't act, they react. They do what they are told. 'Yes sir,' 'no, sir,' always with a snappy salute; but what's behind those eyes?

What's between those ears? Sometimes I have felt as though I were commanding a machine. It's frightening."

Chapter Six

Puzzle

After Lt. Calley and I got into the details of the book, which was to be a military autobiography to tell his life during the time he spent in the Army, in Vietnam and the court-martial, complications arose.

I had brought a New York "agent," who also called himself a literary packager, in on the book to help us sell the product to the publishers, hardcover and paperback.

Friends of mine in the trade in Manhattan as well

as attorney friends expressed reservations when the man took tapes and records I had obtained from Calley.

But Rusty didn't seem to mind, as long as we came up with a deal which would make money for both of us. I continued to push for a decent book that would tell the true story and which would neither glamorize nor degrade Calley as a man or as a soldier. I continued to push for all the details, beginning with his childhood and continuing through the time during which we were then living.

In June of 1970 I received a letter from the agent stating that he could not sell the material because I was not well enough known in the industry.

I telephoned Calley at Ft. Benning, informed him of what the agent had said, and Rusty said he believed another writer would be contacted through another source.

I was taken aback, but not terribly shocked. I told him that I would still like to do a book on the My Lai situation, but that it would be through talking to other sources—especially since all of my material had already been used by the agent and Calley. We chatted for a few more minutes, exchanging pleasantries about favorite night spots and restaurants in Columbus and Atlanta.

For a while I was disgusted with the idea of doing a book, but soon young men who had served in Vietnam during March of 1968 started returning. They came through Montgomery and other places where I happened to be; inevitably I began meeting them.

Some conversations went throughout nights. Others lasted only a few short minutes. But little by little the jigsaw puzzle of Calley, My Lai and the entire affair began to take shape.

Suddenly I could see him more clearly than I ever had before.

I had been too close. But now I had backed away. I began seeing him and the entire situation through a different set of eyes. Everything was put into a wider perspective. And it came alive.

Chapter Seven

The Scene

The Song My villages sat in a basin where rice grew plentifully when the people were there to till the fields, cultivate and harvest the crops. It was the agricultural area of the north central coastland of South Vietnam.

For more than two decades the people of the villages had been ready for any invading forces of foreigners. While they were not working the fields between the green-foilage-covered hills they were busy preparing for the armies that would come.

In Pinkville, the most populated area on a long peninsula which ran parallel to the coast of the South China Sea, an intricate system of underground tunnels for offensive and defensive maneuvers had been constructed throughout the years of fighting the French, Vietcong and finally the Americans.

The villages, which could be called a suburban portion of Pinkville, lay to the west of the greatest populated area. Separating Pinkville and the villages was a wide but shallow body of water.

About three hundred persons lived within the Song My village area. Five hamlets were in the group: My Lai One, Two, Three, Four and Five.

In them lived the farmers of this modern fiefdom. Between the thatch-roofed huts and the concrete-and-straw houses were pens for animals, goats, pigs, oxen, water buffalo and other animals.

Far to the west, beyond miles of rice paddies which bloom a bright green in the spring, not unlike the color of wild onions, are the mountains where Calley was posted when he first came to Vietnam.

He had been in the country little more than a month when he was moved into this more-or-less flatland country for what was called Task Force Barker.

Calley and the rest of C Company had a mission:

wipe out the Vietcong stronghold. But that was not easily done.

C Company joined two other companies at Landing Zone Dottie on a hill northwest of Pinkville in Quang Ngai province on Highway One which ran north to Da Nang and Hue.

On that high ground from which a guard could see the sea to the east and the enemy territory to the southeast Calley first met Capt. Ernest Medina.

Medina was a solemn-faced, tight-lipped professional soldier of Mexican-American origin. Nicknamed "Mad Dog" Medina by his troops, he strutted about the camp staring at his new officers and attempting to make them look like fools.

While stationed on LZ Dottie that night, Medina called Calley "Young Thing," probably because of his baby-faced appearance, and saw that Calley did not take the joke.

After mess that evening, Medina joked about his "Children officers," and he attempted to trip Calley when the young officer left the tent.

Calley fell against the tent flap and did not tumble to the floor.

Medina stared at him, giving him that tough Indian look of self-assurance.

Calley said nothing. He straightened himself and left the quarters.

Afterwards Medina knew that the slightest gesture would embarrass Calley, whom he had spotted as the most sensitive of the group of lieutenants.

And from that moment on he and Calley never got along. Calley continued to praise him and does now. "Medina is a great officer. He's a beautiful man who does the right thing at the right time. He knew how to get his men ready for a big battle, and he got us ready," he said.

However, some of the men in the company told me "sometimes you could see Calley seething after Mad Dog called him Sweet Thing or Sweetheart or anything like that in front of the men of Calley's platoon. You could actually see the red come onto Calley's face sometimes and his eyes would sort of jump around nervously."

But Medina was tough. He'd bark out orders and the men knew that he meant what he said. Calley and the other lieutenants listened to him implicitly when he gave an order.

At that time he had been in the infantry 12 years. Born in 1936 in Springer, New Mexico, of a ne'er-do-well family, he planned to make the Army a career.

In 1952 he joined the National Guard when he lied about his age. Then he went into the Army.

He graduated with honors from the Officers' Candidate School at Ft. Benning in 1964. For two years he remained on the Georgia post as an instructor. In

1966 he was made a captain. When he took over C Company in 1968 he had been a company commander for two years.

Medina loved succeeding. And he wanted to win the shooting match which lay ahead with the VC's in the bottomlands in front of them. It would be a grueling time for two months, but he wanted to put a feather in his cap by chalking up a victory for his company.

There was no better way to carry out such a mission than to sit back and wait. Go about doing your day by day job. Don't get into trouble. Keep your men happy and satisfied. Keep them on their toes. Then when the iron got really hot, strike quickly.

Those were the game plans—and they could have worked.

Calley had mixed feelings about Medina.

About him he said, "Medina was a great, beautiful soldier. He'd always give us hell. He had been an enlisted man for six years before he went to OCS and became an officer. He felt extremely proud of himself for coming up through the ranks.

"He was really a funny guy. Medina was always getting his left and right hands mixed up. He'd think I was the leader of Second Platoon and Brooks the First. It was really the opposite.

"Sometimes he'd call me and give me Brooks' orders. When he finished, I said, 'But Captain, the Second Platoon belongs to Brooks.'

" 'Don't tell me that, shithead'—he always called his platoon leaders 'shithead' and if he didn't you'd know you were in trouble—'follow my orders.'

" 'But I'm Calley, not Brooks, and I'm the leader of First Platoon—not Second,' I insisted.

" 'If you don't want to do it like I want to do it, shithead, do it any fucking way you want,' and he'd stalk off. He never admitted he was wrong.

"One time Brooks and I were in a sweep formation. Our platoons were abreast, covering the territory, then the Third Platoon was behind us. Medina was with the Third.

"Over the horn, he told me, 'Move left!'

"But I knew he was wrong. I knew he meant to move right, because if I moved left I'd be hitting Brooks' platoon—which was already on my left. So, instead of following his order, I moved my men right, away from Brooks' platoon.

"About this time Medina called Brooks and said, 'Where are you going?'

"Brooks answered that he wasn't going anywhere, that he was remaining in a straight line, as ordered.

"Medina then barked over the horn to me, 'Move left! Can't you hear?'

"So I continued to move to the right.

"He called Brooks back and said, 'Move your men to the right,' and then told me again, 'Move your men to the left—and I mean left!'

"At that time, seeing what was going to happen, I shrugged and played along. I ordered my men to the left. Brooks had already given his men the order to move right. And within five minutes our men were walking into each other.

"Medina shouted over the horn, 'Calley! Brooks! Move your men straight ahead into enemy territory!' And we did, bringing them back into the formation we had had before he began giving his orders."

C Company moved out for LZ Uptight the day after it arrived. Uptight was another high ground spot which had been held by another army at another time years before. It was about 30 miles northeast of LZ Dottie toward the coast. After being on the trail two days, the lieutenants, including Calley, learned the mission.

After the first offensive of Tet, the Americans had cut off the Ho Chi Minh Trail which was the supply line from North Vietnam to the VC's in the south.

All intelligence said that the trail had been completely severed, at least temporarily.

But supplies were coming in somewhere, and probably two or three spots along the South China Sea coastline. One of the key spots for VC supplies was Pinkville, intelligence had reported.

At night, hidden along the heavily jungled coastline of the northern portion of South Vietnam, Chinese-type junks would be floated down. Or they would go out to sea and come in at night.

Then the supplies would be taken in a crisscross fashion to the mountains where they would again be distributed to keep alive the Cong offensive.

This supply source needed to be stopped as soon as possible.

From Uptight the C Company would work in semi-circular patterns to the north and west of Pinkville and the Song My villages. Small patrols would go out. They would skirt the territory and watch for supply lines and gather details for a major assault.

The major attack was planned to do away with the supply lines. And it would also finish off the 48th Batallion of the Vietcong army, a tough group of fighting men who had done much damage during the hottest part of Tet.

Calley was leading a patrol into the rice paddies one afternoon when they drew their first fire.

"We all thought we had been shot," said one of the troops. "We hit the water. I believe Lt. Calley hit the water quicker than any of us.

"But soon he was up on his elbows and looking out to see if anyone had been hit.

"No one had been.

"But it was the next day when we were going through a village that the next fire came. I was behind the lieutenant when I heard a sound from one of the little adobe houses.

"I said, 'Psst, hey, Lieutenant. . .

"He turned around toward me and we saw this person duck and run from one building to another.

"No one fired after the figure. We thought it was somebody who had gotten frightened. But in a minute fire came from the building. We fell back against a wall. We were closing in on the house, each of us on opposite sides.

"A grenade rolled out and across the cobblestones. Calley, he turned away and ducked against a doorway across the street, getting out of the way just in the nick of time.

"When the explosion went off the figure broke and ran from the building.

"I lowered my rifle and fired. I made a perfect hit right in the center of the back.

"We went up to the person. I reached down and turned the body over.

"Staring up at me was a pretty pair of dark almond-shaped eyes. She was about 16 years old, I guess. Just about the age of my sister back home. I stared back at her.

"Calley slapped me on the back and said, 'Let's get the shit out of here.' I didn't move for a second or two, still looking into the face of the dead girl. Finally he hit me harder and I took off.

"That night I couldn't eat my chow. I puked my guts out instead. I couldn't stand to think about it, and it hurts even now. It's not that I did it and it's not right and proper, because if I hadn't she might have killed me or some other American soldier. So in my action I might have saved somebody else. But what I ask myself now is, why in the hell are we over there making a 21-year-old American kid a killer and a 16-year-old Vietnamese girl his victim? Why? Hell, man, I'm a veteran, going to school on the GI Bill, but sometimes I think about demonstrating with the hippies. I hate war much more than they can ever possibly imagine."

The patrols from C Company continued their meticulous patrols. They combed the banks of the rivers and the flat rice paddies north of Pinkville and the Song My hamlets.

Alpha Company, based at LZ Dottie, worked closer to the villages and even touched on My Lai Five during one patrol.

A former member of that company who was there on the day said, "It was a tiny place actually, like hundreds of other places I had seen along the coast.

"You can imagine it: tiny houses made of gray mortar, sort of like Mexican houses down in Tijuana; some red brick with little porches; green bushes and trees all over; a few grass-roofed places; little huts scattered here and there for the farm animals; there was even a cow wandering through the streets.

"We went in with rifles ready. Part of our patrol hung back to secure the outer perimeter. Of course, this was no assault. We were checking it out as an intelligence measure.

"All we found were two or three dozen women, mama san types, and about a dozen children.

It looked as innocent as any village in Southern California. More so. It was nothing but a dirty, rural village filled with women and children. Damn, none of us thought it was anything else.

"Our lieutenant reported what we found.

"You have to realize that at the same time other patrols in A Company were edging closer and closer to Pinkville from the west and from the south. They came back more haggard than we did. They came back with reports of gunfire when they got too close to the populated area.

"It seemed then like a game we were playing. It was touch-and-go, hide-and-seek.

"When our ships came in too close on the seaside, the same thing would happen. They had big artillery in the gunworks around the city, and all you had to do was give them a reason to use it and they'd open up. Sometimes at night we'd hear the big guns blasting away at something. We'd hear it all the way to Dottie.

"We'd lay awake and listen. I know I'm not the only one. The other guys were just as frightened as I was. We'd whisper in the night about when we had to go in there. We knew it had to be some time soon. But we kept thinking about that little village with the women and children. That would be easy. All you had to do was walk in. No sweat.

"But all the time we were listening to the blasting of the big guns, and we knew Pinkville was something else again.

"I had a buddy named Harold Hill. He was a PFC, had been caught by the draft when he forgot to register for school in time. He was 19 years old but had already become a man up in the mountains.

"Hill and I were in the same platoon. We toughed out two or three patrols as close as My Lai Three. We passed through My Lai Four the same day.

"Four was not much different from any one of the others. Two was the biggest. It was closest to the river and Pinkville. It had the same type of houses and the women and the children—only more of them. And there was livestock all around.

"That day when we got to Three both of us sensed a danger. It was probably in the air to the entire patrol. I know we could smell it and feel it.

"Hill drew over close to me and said, 'Man, there's going to be some shit thrown at us today. We better stick close.'

"I nodded, and from then on we didn't take our eyes from those openings without doors in the buildings along the dusty streets in the town.

"We were three-fourths of the way through the town when the sound of a grenade exploding rumbled behind us.

"We turned and looked back, and as soon as we did a little gook came out of a doorway and started opening fire.

"The lieutenant and a sergeant hit the ground in front of us.

"I made it to a doorway and went down inside. When I looked back into the street I saw Hill had been shot. He was caught in the leg.

"The lieutenant opened up on the gook, but, by that time two more VC's had joined the party.

"I saw Hill's face turn into the most agonizingly frightened look I've ever seen. I mean, he knew he was going to die right there, and I couldn't stand it.

"He looked at me, his eyes wet, his mouth twisted down, his teeth biting into his lower lip, and I went to him.

"Somehow in the run of no more than about ten feet I brought down the first Charley. I had opened fire as I stepped out. Luckily, I hit him without really aiming.

"As soon as I got to Hill, another bullet hit him in the shoulder, missing me by no more than a foot.

"I reached down and took a hold under his good arm, and he gasped with the hurt.

"I drug him away across the street to the shelter, the lieutenant and the sergeant trying to hold cover for us, but the fire kept on peppering around our feet as we made it.

"Inside the doorway I screamed for a medic when I got Hill propped up against the grimy wall.

"His head fell to one side slightly, and he said, 'Man, I feel like shit,' and he never moved again on his own.

"I closed his eyes and felt sick all the way back to our camp that night. I lay awake and looked at the stars. I think I tried to count them, I don't know. I tried to do everything to keep from thinking about the look on his face. I had never seen anybody die before."

Three days later Alpha Company was told they would be on an assault mission. Their duty would be to penetrate Pinkville. Go through the villages, where the women and children would be evacuated, and hit Pinkville.

C Company would flank them to the north and Bravo Company would come up from the south.

The word was: Go!

Medina told his men they should have initiative. To give them a "strong incentive," he gave them an arm patch of skull-and-crossbones. He told C Company they would be known as "The Death Dealers."

Chapter Eight

First Assaults

Task Force Barker had been in operation about a month when the order for attack came.

Alpha Company had been briefed the night before. Helicopters would take them to a spot near the Song My hamlets. They would move in as quickly as possible. All friendly elements would be removed from the villages.

Follow the attack zone from village to village.

Stand pat and ready on the bank of the river where artillery would be set up.

C Company and B Company would be moving in on their respective flanks.

When everything was ready, A Company would move into Pinkville.

That was the plan.

But the morning came and the men did not react like robots.

Calley's job was to lead an advance patrol onto a small peninsula north of the Song My villages and to a point which overlooked the northernmost section of Pinkville.

A young troop in Calley's platoon later said, "We didn't know what we were doing or where we were going. And that includes Lt. Calley.

"We left our camp and headed south. We had been briefed on our mission, but Calley kept taking out his map and compass and putting them on the ground and checking and double-checking. He called over Sgt. (David) Mitchell several times. Mitchell would look at the map and the compass and would show the way. Hell, Calley couldn't even read the map.

"We were in elephant grass up over our heads, and we had to find our way to the position where we could hold Pinkville intact.

"C Company had three positions to hold to keep the Cong from escaping. And we had to have these positions to give Alpha complete support. But it was late, and we still had not found our position," said the young private from Cleveland, Ohio.

In the meantime, Alpha Company was unloaded between the two outermost villages.

"The choppers dropped us in the open field. I was sure we looked like perfect targets. We cut across the open expanse and made for cover in some tall grass. Not a shot was fired.

"Overhead we had sufficient air cover. They were ready to go, gunners manning their tools, the pilots hovering.

"We regrouped and went toward the villages, one platoon after the other, just as the briefing had called for.

"Still no shots were fired. The villages seemed deserted.

"Between Four and Three, moving toward Pink-ville, we ran up against a tall field of grass. Slowly we made our way through.

"There was a platoon in front of mine. They were moving about as fast as a group of ants.

"Finally they got to the other side and moved out swiftly, guns alert, ready.

"The first mine went off no more than 30 feet in front of me.

101

"A radioman screamed as his body was sliced down the middle. Parts to the radio flew. Blood gushed like a geyser.

"Another went off. Then another.

"Chain reaction.

"I didn't have time to be sick. We gathered on the edge of the field.

"Still not a shot was fired. The two platoons of us left squatted in the grass and waited.

"There was heavy fire to the north and we could hear explosions somewhere in the south."

By this time Calley had pushed his men into a position, but according to Spec. 4 Ansley Morrison "the group was at least a half-mile off-target.

"It was so confused, Pinkville could have poured like a funnel to the north, even if Alpha had succeeded in their attack.

"Instead of getting us onto a peninsula and securing a position to hold the Cong in, he took us out across the river toward an island.

"We went behind a levee to the island, where we suddenly found that we were surrounded on three sides by Cong.

"And the fire started coming from all sides. We dug in. It was like a bunch of frightened animals, the way we hit that dirt and went down. We had to

hold for our lives. And we didn't really have anything to shoot back at, they were hidden so well.

"It was their turf, and it was made clear all the
way to the bottom of your gut."

Headquarters at LZ Dottie was getting word from
Bravo Company which was to come in from the
south and block the opening in that direction.

"Get ready," they were told.

When they moved in, mines started doing the
work of a hundred rifles.

"I can't move!" the word came back.

"What?"

"I'm surrounded. By mines."

Half of Bravo Company had been lost in a matter
of minutes.

"No way to pull out," headquarters was told.

Within minutes the radio announced that Pinkville had opened fire on Alpha Company, which
was still stranded in the elephant grass.

Alpha was firing back, but the company was not
getting the support it needed from Charlie Company.

"What the hell's happened to Medina?"

But Medina couldn't get his men in order. They were scattered along the northern borders of the river, and Calley's platoon was on an island without cover except for the dirt and mud piled around them.

The situation in the early afternoon looked not only hopeless, the entire operation appeared to be a complete failure.

In mid-afternoon, when Alpha started to pull out to retreat to the helicopter landing field, they caught more fire from My Lai Four.

"We thought the village was deserted. But when we turned to run to the choppers, we were caught in crossfire.

"My Lai Four and Five had people with guns, and we were in the middle.

"Another half of our men were lost before we could get away.

"And as we were lifted, the entire bright afternoon sky was filled with smoke and rifle shots from the east and from below.

"We were tired and disillusioned and totally whipped, and I don't think I've ever felt lower. It had been Death Day."

Medina told Calley to pull off the island. He and

his men would have to break and run, keeping their heads below the levee between them and the mainland.

"Calley called for more support, but he was apparently ignored by Medina.

"We ran like hell, one after the other, through the shallow water and crawled as quickly as possible behind the levee to keep from being hit.

"The fire came hot as we skittered across and took our places back on the land and tried to keep the fire away from those to come.

"When Calley came the radioman was with him, and he was hit and blown to kingdom come before they even made it to the levee.

"The sergeant had been with us, and he kept us moving, and told us what to do, then he helped Calley to us.

"The lieutenant came to us and told us what had happened, and it was about dark when we headed back.

"Shit!"

During the next month a few patrols went out, new plans were organized, some minor wounds healed and some of the men, including Calley, went on weekend leaves to nearby cities.

The Making of a Hero

On routine patrols several men were killed. But mostly it was rest and waiting.

The next assault took place during the first week of March.

Charlie Company had approximately the same mission to carry out: block Pinkville from the north. And Calley's platoon had to go to the same spot it had been assigned to previously. This time the lieutenant found the peninsula. His men were ready shortly after six a.m. They were waiting.

Bravo Company had the strike zone of the Song My villages this time.

Again My Lai Five and Six appeared deserted. A platoon checked them out. No one was found.

The company proceeded as planned, careful to watch for mines.

As soon as the men got into position to move into My Lai Four, fire came from behind them. They had overlooked someone in the village.

But it was more than one. It had to be more than one.

Several men in Bravo were hit.

Bravo turned and faced Five, readied to fire. Then shots came from My Lai Four. The VC had gotten in early or the night before. They had dug in and had become as ready as they could be.

Bravo was caught from both sides. One man after another fell.

"There was no attack," one soldier said later. "We got the shit knocked out of us, and the only thing to do was to pull out as fast as we could. And we did."

In the south, Alpha Company, which had been replenished with new troops, lost about 25 per cent in the mine fields.

By 10 o'clock that morning the men were on their way back to camp.

The next time, they knew, would be different.

Chapter Nine

Briefing

If "Mad Dog" Medina was pissed off at the failure of the first attack, he was angered at the second foul-up. But he couldn't blame his men this time.

He was proud of the way his troops had acted in the second try, and now he knew Charlie Company would be able to do the job as he imagined it should be done.

"When you go into a Goddam place like that you can't look back," one troop said he told him on LZ

Uptight as they were waiting to be called as the assaulting party.

"There should be no reason to look back. If the Army does what it's supposed to do, you wipe out the enemy," the troop quoted his commanding officer.

According to others, Medina was getting ready for the attack as soon as the second assault was finished.

"Ole 'Mad Dog' kind of paced the floor for days and days," said one of his lieutenants.

"He got angry at most of us, but Calley in particular. Any little thing Calley would do wrong, like stump his toe—which he was doing constantly—Medina would shout and scream and curse and make Calley nervous as hell.

"Medina sent Calley and his platoon out on patrol into the north several times during this period. Each time they caught fire and came back with casualties.

"The whole damn unit of men were scared as hell by the end of two weeks, by the time they had waited, by the time they'd seen blood and had been shot at almost constantly.

"It wasn't like they were the finest trained troops in the world. They weren't. Most of us had been in Vietnam little more than three months by that time. Task Force Barker was our first experience with real live fire. We hadn't seen people dying around us, and a lot of the troops sat around during those days and stared at the sky or other troops or buildings. I know they were trying to understand what was happening. They were trying to realize all of this was a part of life. Not a part of life they were used to living, but a part of something they had to get used to.

"They sure as hell weren't ready to go back into combat. Not at that stage of the game. But I don't guess that was for me to say. Like one of the old troops told me one time, 'You kids are spoiled rotten. Who the hell ever heard of hot rations in the field?' But you know something? That's what we demanded, and that's what we got. Too bad we didn't ask for the end of that shitty thing before now, we'd have probably gotten that too."

On the day before they were to travel down bowling lane attack alley Sgt. George Cox was killed on patrol. His body was brought into the encampment at LZ Dottie, where C Company now made its base. The funeral would be that evening, and Medina would say a few words over the body.

That evening at twilight, the body in its temporary wooden coffin, flag draped over the box, the group of men gathered around.

111

Hat in hand, the dark-haired, Indian-faced captain spoke his words barely above a whisper.

His voice broke with emotion as he said what a fine lad the soldier had been and how bravely he had died.

The troops of C Company kept their heads bowed. They kept their eyes peeled on the top of the coffin.

And Medina said that they would avenge the death of the young man on the battlefield in the morning. And he added that tomorrow, March 16, 1968, would be the boy's day.

More than a half-dozen of the troops gathered there said later that Medina announced that "everything that moves in the villages will be killed. The Cong, who killed our friend, will be wasted."

Then quietly, sadly, mournfully, the troops made their way back to the hooches where they were to sleep that night.

The lieutenants followed Medina to a more technical briefing.

That briefing became one of the most controversial points in the subsequent court-martial of Lt. Calley at Ft. Benning.

During his testimony Medina said he told Calley and others that they would be up against some of the toughest fighting men, the 48th Batallion of Vietcong, when they entered My Lai Four the next day.

He said he told them they would be outnumbered two-to-one. "I told them that even though we were outnumbered, that we had doubled coverage of gunships that were being provided, and that the artillery was being placed on the village. And that they would help make up for the difference in ratio between the enemy forces and our company.

"The briefing that I conducted for my company was that C Company had been selected to conduct a combat assault operation into the village of My Lai Four beginning with LZ time 0600 hours on the morning of the 16th of March of 1968.

"I gave them the enemy situation, intelligence reports—good intelligence reports that the 48th VC Battalion was located at the village of My Lai Four.

"I told them what the VC battalion was approximately—numbered approximately 250 to 280 men and that we would be outnumbered two-to-one and what we could expect too—a hell of a good fight and that we would probably be heavily engaged.

"The intelligence reports also indicated that the innocent civilians or noncombatants would be gone to market at 0700 hours in the morning. This was one reason why the artillery preparation was being placed on the village at 0720 hours, with the combat assault LZ time 0730 hours. I did not make any reference to the handling of prisoners."

In direct testimony, in answer to questions asked by the Army's chief prosecutor, Capt. Aubrey Daniel, Medina said, "One of the questions that was asked of me at the briefing was, 'Do we kill women and children?' My reply to that question was, 'No, you do not kill women and children. You must use common sense. If they have a weapon and are trying to engage you, you can shoot back, but you must use common sense."

And he continued, again answering Daniel's questions, "There were no instructions given as far as the capture or collection of any noncombatants in the village of My Lai Four. It was standard procedure in other operations that we had conducted that the sweep elements, when they moved through the village, would move through as rapidly as possible, pushing any inhabitants to the far side of the village, collecting them in an open area."

When asked if he ordered the men to "kill everything that moved," he answered, "No, sir."

When Calley testified a different story was told. He was asked by his defense counsel, George Latimer, "Do you recall Capt. Medina telling you there would be no women and children in the village?"

Calley answered, "No, sir, I don't. I don't remember him saying there would be no women and children in the village, sir. He said that the next morning we would be going in to assault Pinkville, that it was our mission to keep up a high speed— keep up a high speed momentum of attack. Not to let anyone get behind us."

"Did he make any comments about the civilians, as to what they might be?" Latimer asked.

And Calley responded, "Well, the only remark he made as to civilians, about civilians, was that all civilians had left the area, there were no civilians in the area. And anyone there would be considered enemies."

According to Seymore Hersh in his book "My Lai 4," one of the men told the Criminal Investigating Division that Medina "ordered us to 'kill everything in the village.' The men in my squad talked about this among ourselves that night because the order . . . was so unusual. We all agreed that Medina meant for us to kill every man, woman and child in the village."

Another said the captain said that when the company left the area "nothing would be walking, growing or crawling," Hersh reported.

Sgt. William Logan of Shreveport, La., said that when he and his buddies went to bed that night they lay awake for a long while. They talked in whispers about what was coming the next morning and said that they would be ready to wipe out the entire coast after what Medina had told them.

Logan said that it was very dark when one of the young officers came into their hooch and sat down in the middle of the floor.

"He pulled a pouch from the pocket of his clothes, took a packet of paper and tore off a sheet and began rolling a cigarette in the slight moonlight.

"We all watched him like he was crazy or something. Every once in a while he'd look around at us and grin and maybe giggle or something. He didn't say a word until the weed had been rolled.

"When he finished he held out the weed and said 'You guys want a drag? This is the best stuff in 'Nam.'

"He lit it up and took a deep drag and passed it around to about three of us.

"We finished it off and cut another.

"By the time we got through with the second I was ready to sleep forever and ever. I fell back to sleep as soon as he got up and went off singing a song. The others were still talking when I closed my eyes.

"That lieutenant never made it through the war, but he had the right idea about how to get through a night out there. I mean, we were so psyched up we couldn't sleep. But after the grass, it was easy. And I know we weren't the only ones doing that thing. It was everywhere.

"That stuff was as easy to come by as Luckies, and it wasn't much more expensive than regular cigarettes. Hell, they used to come out with the stuff packed in duffle bags. It's wild!"

Chapter Ten

My Lai

They didn't stop to look back. They knew there was no need to look back. Everything behind them looked like Atlanta after Sherman.

At 7:20 a.m. a frightened group of young men boarded the helicopter at LZ Dottie led by 24-year-old Lt. William Calley.

A few minutes later the copter landed in what had been described to them as a "hot" area, but according to the troops there was no fire in the area when they unloaded.

Calley took the men quickly through the field with mud over their ankles.

Although no fire came from the hamlet, less than a half-mile away, the men went in firing at everything they saw.

"It didn't take us any time to have the place secured and in our control. I don't know how many people were shot during those first few minutes, but I would suspect at least 30 or 40. I saw that many myself," said Charles Sledge, Calley's radioman.

Paul Meadlo later said that he saw a "gook standing up and shaking and waving his arms and then he was shot."

"I saw this one old sonofabitch standing next to a well and somebody hollered that he was a VC and one of the other guys said something and another said, 'Shoot the sonofabitch,' and somebody did," said another of the troops.

"Some guy was in a rice field, doing something to a rice plant. He looked up and he got it. That was the most confused operation I ever went on. Just everything was screwed up.

"I looked around for Lt. Calley and couldn't find him. Finally when I did see him he didn't know any more than anybody else. I thought he was going to lead us out of there, get us out of the killing, but he just pulled his trigger and shot into a ditch full of people," said Allen Boyce.

According to another soldier, he heard the firing of rifles the moment he got off the helicopter behind Calley's platoon. He had never been in a "hot" firing zone before, and "This got their adrenalin going."

At his court-martial Calley said, "I heard a considerable volume of firing to my north, and I moved up along the edge of the ditch and around a hooch and I broke out in a clearing and my men had a number of Vietnamese in the ditch and were firing on them."

His attorney, Latimer, asked him: "What did you do after you saw them shooting in the ditch?"

"Well, I fired into the ditch also, sir."

"Prior to that time, had you received any other messages from Capt. Medina?"

"Still to hurry up and get my men out in position where they were supposed to be, sir."

"Did you leave the vicinity of the ditch shortly thereafter—after you fired in the ditch, when did you leave it, was it shortly or did you stay there a long while, a short time or what did you do?"

"I don't take it as . . . it was a very rapid period of time to me. I can't say basically what time it was. It seems like it was only a matter of a half-minute, maybe a full minute at the most, when the men started moving across."

"Did you have a chance to look and observe what was in the ditch?"

"Yes, sir. Dead people, sir."

"Did you see any appearance of anybody being alive in there?"

"No, sir."

"At any time that you were alone and near that ditch, did you push or help anybody push people into the ditch?"

"Yes and no, sir. When I came out of this hedge-row, I came right up to about the last man to go into the ditch. I didn't physically touch him, but if he would have stopped I guess I would have."

"Did he . . . was somebody there with him to order him in or push him in?"

"They had been ordered in . . . to go in the ditch, sir."

"Do you know who gave them that information?"

"Well, indirectly, I did, sir. I had told Meadlo to get them on the other side of the ditch, sir."

"Aside from what you have said about the shooting into the ditch, was there any other shooting you did in that general vicinity?"

"The next time I fired . . . I started walking out to this machinegun position and I fired on a head moving through the rice. I just saw a head moving through the rice and fired. One of my RTOs (radiomen) went over and checked it out.

"It was just a small boy."

"Did you know that at the time you shot?"

"No, sir."

"There has been some testimony in the record, and do you have a recollection of an incident that happened which has been described, I think, by some witnesses of the event as a monk, do you recall that?"

"I have heard of the incident, yes, sir."

"Did you participate in an incident such as that?"

"Not with a monk that I know of. A man was brought up to me for interrogation and I interrogated him briefly. I butt-stroked him in the mouth, sir. It knocked him down."

"Did you shoot him?"

"No, sir, I did not."

"Did he eventually get in the ditch, to your knowledge?"

"Yes, sir, he eventually ended up in the ditch."

"What propelled him into the ditch?"

"I believe somebody's foot, sir."

"Was it yours?"

"No, sir, it wasn't."

"Let me ask you another—your impressions of another incident. There has been some testimony in the record to the effect that there was a child running from the ditch, that you threw him back in the ditch and you shot him. Did you participate in any such event?"

"No, sir, I did not."

"Did you see a boy or a child running from the ditch?"

"No, sir, I did not. Wait! Let me backtrack. Now this child that I supposedly said I shot was running away from the ditch but it is not in the same location. It is east of the ditch but I was running away from the ditch."

"To the extent that you shot and it turned out ultimately to be a child, is that the only impression you have of any incident which involved a child?"

"Yes, sir."

"There has been some information disclosed that you heard before the court that you stood there at the ditch for a considerable period of time, that you waited and had your troops organized, groups of Vietnamese thrown in the ditch and knocked them down in the ditch or pushed them in the ditch and that you fired there for approximately an hour and a half as those groups marched up. Did you participate in any such a shooting or any such an event?"

"No, sir. I did not. Like I said, I gave the order to take those people through the ditch and had also told Meadlo if he couldn't move them to waste them as I directed. Other than that there was only that one incident. I never stood up there for any period of time. The main mission was to get my men on the other side of the ditch and get in that defensive position and that is what I did, sir."

"Now why did you give Meadlo a message or the order that if he couldn't get rid of them to waste them?"

"Because that was my order, sir. That was the order of the day, sir."

"Who gave you that order?"

"My commanding officer, sir, Capt. Medina, sir."

"And stated in that posture, in substantially those words, how many times did you receive such an order from Capt. Medina?"

"The night before in the company briefing, platoon leaders' briefing, the following morning before we lifted off and twice there in the village."

"I am going to ask you this. During the operation, My Lai Four, did you intend specifically to kill Vietnamese man, woman and child?

"No, sir, I did not."

"How did you intend on that occasion to waste something?"

"To waste or destroy the enemy, sir. To go into the area and destroy the enemy that were designated and that is it. I went into the area to destroy the enemy, sir. I never sat down to analyze it, men, women, and children. They were enemy and just people."

"And were you motivated by other things besides the fact that those were the enemy? Did you have some other reasons for treating them that way altogether? I am talking now about your briefings. Did you get any information out of that?"

"Well, I was ordered to go in there and destroy the enemy. That was my job on that day. That was the mission I was given. I did not sit down and think in terms of men, women and children. They were all classified the same, and that was the classification that we dealt with, just as enemy soldiers."

"Who gave you that classification the last time you got it?"

"Capt. Medina, sir."

"Did he classify in any of his briefings as to whether the enemy would include men, women and children?"

"Not specifically in that briefing, he didn't break it down and say the enemy will encompass that. We had been talking about it from the time we got there, that men, women and children were enemy soldiers."

Calley and his men did indeed destroy My Lai Four on that day in mid-March.

And according to Meadlo's emotional confession

on television, Medina and Calley "passed each other quite a few times that morning, but didn't say anything.

"I don't know if the CO gave the order to kill or not, but he was right there when it happened." He went on to say that Medina stood by and watched without concern while some of the killing was going on before his eyes.

And other soldiers at My Lai stated that Medina shot a Vietnamese woman and teenager.

And Jay Roberts, a reporter with the Army's 31st Public Information Detachment, said later that Medina directed the action in the village for at least two hours during the morning.

Gary Garfolo said, "Every time I saw Calley he was running from one end of the village to the other. I don't know what was wrong with the guy, or the rest of us, but we didn't do too much that was logical."

Garfolo took someone else's grenade launcher and with it shot and killed a water buffalo.

During the court-martial Ronald Haeberle, a combat photographer who was sent with Roberts to the scene of the battle, said, "It seemed like quite a large group of people. I'd estimate between 50 and 75. I noticed these people squatting in the Vietnamese position I noticed about five soldiers. I saw three or four people walking. I thought nothing of it. Then I heard firing and I could see some of the people trying to get up and run. They just fell down again. One woman was trying to make it, trying to run, with a baby in her arms." He added that no one was left standing when the firing stopped. And he said he did not see Calley in this group of soldiers.

Also at the court-martial was Rennard Doines of Fort Worth, Texas, who had been 20 years old at the time of the My Lai massacre. He described the killing of livestock and dogs on the entrance into the hamlet.

Afterwards, he said that he and others took ten to 15 prisoners from thatch-roofed hooches. "Most of them were women, children and old men, trying to hide," he explained.

They were escorted to Calley, and Doines returned to the village. When he returned to the spot where he had left the prisoners with Calley, "I went over there and looked and there was a bunch of dead people; about ten or 15 dead people. Most of them were little kids, babies like, and old women. They were lying there, bleeding."

And Jeffery LaCross of Big Rapids, Michigan, the second lieutenant who led C Company's Third Platoon which followed Calley's group said he talked to Medina about four times and the captain said, "make sure to take our time, make a thorough search and don't miss anything. He said we had gunships overhead and had plenty of time to do a good job."

Another witness for the prosecution at Calley's court-martial was Robert Maples of Freehold, New Jersey. He had been a machinegunner in Calley's platoon when he was 19 years old.

He testified that a group of Vietnamese people went into a ditch willingly when Calley told them, and then Calley asked him to use his machine gun.

"What did you do?" asked Daniels.

"I refused," Maples answered.

"You can't remember the rest of the conversation?"

"No."

"Were any of these people armed?"

"No."

"Was there any hostile fire?"

"No."

Later Maples said he witnessed Calley and Meadlo firing into the ditch at the people.

At the court-martial, Meadlo, who had been a 20-year-old private first class at the time of the My Lai incident, said that after the First Platoon entered the hamlet, "We just gathered up people and started leading them to a designated area. They were between the ages of 30 and 50, the men, women."

Daniels asked, "Why did you gather the people up?"

"Because we all expected them to be Vietcong, and as far as I'm concerned they're still VC," Meadlo answered.

"What did you do with these people?"

"We led them into a clearing in the center of the village."

"How many people did you have at this time?"

"Oh, about 35 or 40."

"What did you do when you got there?"

"What did I do when I got there? I just guarded them."

"When did you see Lt. Calley?"

"When he came up to me and said, 'You know what to do with them Meadlo.' I assumed he meant guard them, and I said yes."

"Did any of them have any weapons?"

"Not that we could observe."

When asked to describe the prisoners, he said that some were women with babies in their arms.

Calley returned to the scene where he was guarding the prisoners and said to Meadlo, "How come they're not dead?"

Meadlo said he didn't know Calley wanted them dead.

"I want them dead," Calley said.

Meadlo testified to this exchange under direct examination by the prosecutor at the court-martial.

"He told me to help him shoot them," he said.

"What did you do?"

"I helped him shoot them."

"How many magazines did Calley use?"

"Four or five."

"Did Lt. Calley say anything else to you there?"

"No."

From this location, where he and Calley killed the first Vietnamese, according to his testimony, Meadlo then went to the ditch which Calley had described. It was located on the eastern side of the village.

On the edge of the drainage ditch Calley was waiting with about 75 to 100 people when Meadlo came up, the former PFC said.

"We got another job to do, Meadlo," Calley told him.

"Lt. Calley started shoving them off and shooting them in the ravine," said Meadlo.

"How many times did he shoot?" asked Daniels.

"How many times did he shoot? I can't remember that. He ordered me to help him kill the people so I started shoving them off and shooting them, too."

"How long did you fire?"

"I don't know."

"Did you change magazines?"

"Yes."

"Did Lt. Calley change magazines?"

"Yes, between ten and 15 times."

"Did you see anybody alive when you left?"

"Like I said, I couldn't tell whether they were mortally wounded or not."

And under cross-examination by defense counsel, Meadlo said that the night before the foray Medina had told his men "that there was a Vietcong organization in the village and that everybody there is a VC or a VC sympathizer, and that we were supposed to search and destroy it and that includes men, women and children and livestock."

Earlier Harry Stanley had told the CID, according to Seymore Hersh, that he had seen "some old women and some little children—15 or 20 of them —in a group around a temple where some incense was burning. They were kneeling and crying and praying, and various soldiers . . . walked by and executed women and children by shooting them in the head with their rifles. The soldiers killed all 15 or 20 of them. . . ."

The radio operator, Charles Sledge, told the court of another incident. This one involved Calley's confrontation with a man in monk's robes.

Sledge said the incident occurred near the drainage ditch on the eastern side of the village.

The man was brought to the lieutenant for questioning.

Sledge said, "The priest would say, 'No Viet,' and he held his hands in this shape (as though in prayer). Calley asked him a few more questions and he bowed his head and he still said, 'No Viet.' Then he hit him with the butt of his rifle in the mouth."

"What did the priest do?" asked Daniels.

"He didn't do nothing but fall back, doing this with his hands again, sort of like pleading. Lt. Calley took his rifle at point-blank and pulled the trigger in the priest's face. Half his head was blown off."

Calley's defense counsel asked if the priest could have had a weapon hidden under his white robes. Sledge answered that it was possible.

The attorney for Calley also asked if the prayer-like gesture might have been an attempt to reach for the hidden weapon. Sledge also answered this question in the affirmative.

Sledge also described the scene on the trail leading into the village when Meadlo rounded up the first prisoners.

133

"Lt. Calley went over to them and said a few words to them. They said, 'No Vietcong.' He came back and told Meadlo to waste them."

"What did Meadlo do?" asked Daniels.

"He started shooting."

"What did the people do?"

"A few started falling, then I turned my head."

At another time during the morning, Sledge said, someone saw a child of about two—he didn't remember whether it was a boy or a girl—and the soldier shouted, "There's a child."

Sledge said the "little baby" was running back toward the village away from the drainage ditch.

"Lt. Calley grabbed it by the arm and threw it into the ditch and fired."

"How many shots did he fire?" asked Daniels.

"One," answered Sledge.

Calley later denied both of these incidents in his own testimony.

When defense counsel questioned Sledge, he said he could not see where the round fired at the child hit.

"So you don't even know whether the child was even hit by that round?"

"No, sir," Sledge said.

Thomas Turner, who had been 21 years old and a rifleman in Calley's platoon, testified that he saw Calley fire into the ditch at "a variety of people there—men, women and children" for "approximately an hour and a half."

Turner described the group: "They were squatting in the ditch. Some of them were screaming and crying. There was being brought up small groups of people and they were being placed in the ditch and Lt. Calley was firing into it." And he added that about 90 to 100 persons were in the ditch or shoved into it.

Dennis Conti of Providence, Rhode Island, was with Meadlo when they entered the village and began rounding up prisoners.

"Lt. Calley came out and said, 'Take care of these people.' So we said all right. So we stood there and we watched them.

"Then Lt. Calley came out a few minutes later and said, 'I thought I told you to take care of these people?'

"We said we were, we were guarding them and he said, 'We'll get on line and shoot them.' "

Conti said that he had only a grenade launcher and not a rifle, then Calley and Meadlo began shooting "directly into the people for about two minutes and the people screamed and yelled. I guess they tried to get up. They were pretty messed up. There were a lot of heads blown off."

The young man, who was only 18 years old when the affair took place, said he later walked to the ditch on the other side of the town where he saw Calley and Sgt. David Mitchell firing into a group of people.

"A lot of them were trying to get up. Most were just screaming. They were shot up pretty bad. I looked down and seen a woman try to get up. I seen Lt. Calley fire and blow the side of her head off."

Assistant defense counsel, Richard Kay of Cleveland, Ohio, one of the founders of the American Independent Party in that state, attempted to discredit Conti's testimony.

"Isn't it a fact you were going through My Lai that day looking for women?" asked Kay.

"No," he said.

"Isn't it true that on the day of the killings in My Lai you were smoking marijuana that morning?"

"No," he said.

"Isn't it true that you were out to get Lt. Calley because he pulled you off a Vietnamese woman you were raping?"

"No."

"Didn't you put a gun to a baby's head and force his mother to commit an unnatural sex act?"

"No."

Conti appeared at the court-martial with long dark hair, muttonchop sideburns and a mustache.

"Do you remember one night, you were on guard duty and had an M79 (grenade launcher) and you shot all your ammunition so when it came time to go on patrol you didn't have any ammunition left? You remember that night?" Kay asked.

"That's right. I didn't have any ammunition."

"Weren't you mad at Lt. Calley for reporting you?"

"I don't think so."

Altogether five members of First Platoon told details as they had seen them.

James Dursi was the last witness for the prosecution. A 20-year-old rifleman with the outfit, he reiterated some of the earlier testimony. He told of gathering about 15 villagers "mostly old men, women and small children, ranging from babies carried by their mothers to children five to six years old."

He had seen Meadlo and had overheard Calley ask Meadlo to "take care of that group" and had later heard Calley ask Meadlo, "Why haven't you wasted them yet?"

"Meadlo stood there astonished," Dursi said.

137

"As I made a turn in the trail, I heard firing to my rear," he continued.

"What type?" asked Daniels.

"M16 fire."

Dursi moved his group of prisoners through the village until he came to the drainage ditch where he remained until Calley arrived.

"He (Calley) came across first and he was followed by Meadlo. Meadlo was shook up. He was crying.

"Lt. Calley said to Meadlo, 'We have another job to do.' And then he told us to start putting people into the ditch.

"We moved the people into the ditch with our rifles at a port arms position. Some started crying and they were yelling. I was ordered to shoot."

"By whom?" asked Daniels.

"Lt. Calley."

"What did he say?"

"I can't remember the exact wording, something like start firing, something like that.

"Then Lt. Calley and Meadlo started firing into the ditch. Meadlo turned to me shortly after the shooting began and said, 'Shoot! Why don't you fire?'

"He was crying and yelling, I just said, 'I can't, I won't,' and looked down at the ground."

"What were the people doing?" asked Daniels.

"They were screaming and yelling. They were diving on top of one another. Some mothers were trying to protect their children.

"Lt. Calley came up to me and told me to get across the ditch before I got sick. So I moved about 15 feet to my right, and I moved across the ditch. I saw a lot of blood, chest, arms, some head wounds."

"Lt. Calley ordered you to fire?"

"Yes, sir."

"Why did you not fire?"

"I couldn't go through with it—these defenseless men, women, kids."

Why did it continue to happen through the morning? one asks himself.

According to Conti in an interview, "We were all kind of crazed. We were so psyched up we didn't know what we were doing. We went into that village expecting to receive fire. We knew there would be VC troops, and we had to hit first.

Ronald Grzesik told Seymore Hersh, "You get to like them (Vietnamese). I had a little more respect for the average Vietnamese."

When the My Lai Four assault occurred, Grzesik said, "It just started building. I don't know why. Everybody reached the point where they were frustrated. We weren't getting any action, yet the only thing on our mind was survival.

"After Bill (William Weber) got killed, I began to stop caring. I remember writing a letter home saying that I once had sympathy for these people, but now I didn't care. I became passive; I wouldn't beat them up but I wouldn't try to stop it. Yet I told Calley at one point that I wouldn't question anybody unless he stopped beating them up. There'd be days when I'd just be sick of it."

When Lt. Stephen Brooks' second platoon came into My Lai Four, they entered firing.

One of Brooks' men later said, "I felt sick to the bottom of my stomach when we moved through those streets. There were bodies piled up on the edge of town going in, and we didn't know what lay in store for us.

"We had our M16's ready, but little else remained. I remember seeing a little kid lying on a small porch of a brick house. I don't know whether it was a boy or a girl. The face was down. But blood poured from the back. It didn't move.

"Some of the guys in our group fired at the people who were obviously already dead. It just made me sick, and it still makes me sick sometimes when I think about it.

"Even Medina went crazy on that day. He was running back and forth in every direction. I think he was more with us than the other groups. He was looking over everything, and he knew what was going on. He couldn't have been blind that day. He had to see it."

Herbert Carter later told authorities that a woman was spotted and was knocked down. "Medina shot her with his M16 rifle. I was 50 or 60 feet away and saw this. There was no reason to shoot this girl."

Carter also quoted Medina as saying, "Kill every one. Leave no one standing," as the platoons of C Company made their way through the villages.

The two Army correspondents, Haeberle and Roberts, later attempted to report all that they had seen during the day. However, they were told it would not be correct to do such a thing. Troops did not need to be informed of atrocities. And anyway, how could the two of them have seen everything that happened during the day? they were asked.

The two young men said they saw villages burning, completely destroyed; they saw people lying dead in piles; they witnessed dead animals. They said they watched while several soldiers went through a victim's pockets for money or other valuables.

One Second Platoon soldier told this story:

"I was running down the main road toward Calley and the others of the First Platoon when this guy in front of me put his rifle on a crying woman who was standing on the porch of her house.

"The woman was crying and shouting real crazy like, and I stopped in my tracks.

"She had a little boy in her arms. The little boy had been shot and killed by somebody, and she was just going crazy over it.

"I wanted to do something. I didn't know what to do. God!

"That guy in front of me pulled the trigger of his M16 and the woman fell to the ground and the baby tumbled out of her arms.

"I was so scared I didn't know what to do. I was sick.

"The guy opened fire again, like he couldn't get enough of it, and the bullets crashed into the little boy, and blood splattered everywhere. Then he started unloading into the woman.

"I knew I was going to vomit right there on the street. I turned my head and ran by him toward the platoon.

"It was nothing but a Goddam nightmare. A nightmare!"

Chapter Eleven

Thompson

If there was a hero that day it was Chief Warrant Officer Hugh C. Thompson.

A good ole boy from Decatur, Georgia, Hugh Thompson knew tragedy when he saw it happening beneath him as he hovered over My Lai Four on that day in March. And he knew that when a tragic event was taking place, he had to rush in and had to do whatever possible to help the victims of circumstance. He was raised in the middle middle-class, a Baptist, and he didn't believe in watching little folks being pushed around.

Like the news story of Calley's charge, I had been tipped off about the Thompson series of heroic happenings. This tip also came from Washington sources.

Also like the charge, the Army was not free with its information about the circumstances.

Two days before Thanksgiving, 1969, I contacted Thompson via telephone. He was living on Ft. Rucker Army post in south Alabama.

I told him I had been authorized by *Time Magazine* to pay him $300 for his exclusive story for the following week's edition.

An editor at *Time* had contacted me when he discovered through persons in the southeast that I had written the original story about the Calley charges. Also, I had done work for *Time* previously.

Thompson said that he was interested, that he needed the money, but he would have to check with his immediate superiors before telling the story.

He did tell me that he had been contacted by military investigators—I later found out they were CID personnel—and had been asked about details concerning what he knew about an alleged massacre in South Vietnam.

I told him I would be in touch with him the next

day, and we left it at that.

In the meantime, I talked to the *Time Magazine* people as well as to the editors at the *Journal*. All were interested. Here would indeed be a heroic story, if what I had heard was true.

Time authorized me to go as high as $500 if necessary for the story.

But the next morning Thompson said he had been ordered not to talk because he was a possible witness in the upcoming court-martial of Lt. Calley.

I asked if I could visit with him at Ft. Rucker. He said he would be busy that day, but he would be home Thanksgiving.

On Thanksgiving I drove to his home.

The tall, youthful, rawboned handsome helicopter pilot lived in modest surroundings on the post. He was friendly, but very guarded.

I told him *Time* would pay $500 for the story from his point-of-view.

After he heard the words, he grimaced. He said he would like to have the money, that he was in debt and would like to pay off a bank note. But he was quick to add that his career in the Army came first.

Thompson added that while he could say nothing at that time, that it might be interesting to check with the public information officials on the post about an honor he received in October.

With this lead, I remained at nearby Enterprise, Alabama, until the next day, when I went to the Ft. Rucker information office.

There an officer let me look at a file of publicity statements concerning Thompson.

Later that morning, back home in Montgomery, I wrote the story and also read it to an editor at *Time Magazine*.

The *Journal* published the following dispatch on November 29, 1969:

An Army helicopter pilot, said to be the man who halted the Pinkville massacre, has been decorated for rescuing a wounded Vietnamese child in March, 1968.

Warrant Officer Hugh C. Thompson Jr., who refused to answer questions concerning his action in Vietnam because he said he was under direct orders not to talk, was given a Distinguished Flying Cross last month.

Thompson, "while performing a reconnaissance and screening mission, spotted 15 young children attempting to hide in a bunker, landed and evacuated them to a safe area.

"Moments later he located a wounded Vietnamese child. Disregarding his (Thompson's) own safety, he again landed and evacuated the wounded child to Quang Ngan Hospital," the official Army statement read.

Public information officers at Ft. Rucker, Ala., said the action took place on March 16, 1968, during the time of the My Lai village massacre.

When asked the location of the heroic action, Officer Thompson said he could not answer because he was a potential witness in the Ft. Benning, Ga., court-martial of Lt. William L. Calley, now being charged for the murder of 109 South Vietnamese civilians.

A Negro specialist 4th class, Varnado Simpson, of Mississippi, told a reporter that a radio operator said a helicopter pilot, whose name Simpson did not know, watched the Pinkville massacre until "he couldn't stand no more."

At that time the pilot radioed headquarters and reported the incident, Simpson said.

The pilot was then ordered to stop the killing, Simpson said.

Thompson, a 27-year-old career Army man and former student of Troy University (in Alabama), is a native of Decatur, Ga.

He holds the Purple Heart with an Oak Leaf Cluster, Air Medal with 16 Oak Leaf Clusters, Bronze Star, Army Good Conduct Medal, Navy Good Conduct Medal and two Vietnam campaign medals.

Thompson spent six years in the Navy before

entering the Army on June 30, 1966. He was in Vietnam from 1967 until August of 1968, when he was evacuated by medical transport with a compression fracture of the back.

The warrant officer said he could answer no questions concerning his duty in Vietnam, because he is a potential witness.

Lt. Calley has been charged with the murder of 109 South Vietnamese civilians. He reportedly killed men, women, and children in Pinkville, a village in South Vietnam.

Again an obvious attempt by the Army to squelch information had failed.

Later I talked to Thompson, after he had been released as a witness, and to others who were present on the day.

The mission was nothing out of the ordinary for Thompson and the two men who accompanied him in the observation helicopter.

Destination: Pinkville and the Song My villages.

He was with the 123rd Aviation Battalion. And shortly after eight a.m. he and his crew boarded the chopper and headed south.

They arrived at their destination at about nine and radioed back that they saw a VC soldier marching south with a weapon.

Then Thompson guided the copter toward the Song My villages, primarily to lend any assistance, if needed.

"They didn't need my help. I saw that immediately. There were piles of dead people along the sides of roads and in a ditch east of the place."

His immediate reaction to what he saw was to mark the wounded with smoke so they could begin being treated by medics.

"The first one that I marked was a girl that was wounded, and they came over and walked up to her, put their weapon on automatic and let her have it."

Later Thompson identified the man who did the shooting as Captain Medina for the Army Inspector General's office.

Also according to the Inspector General's report, one of Thompson's crew that day, Lawrence M. "Larry" Colburn, a gunner, said the 20-year-old girl "had been wounded in the stomach, I think, or the chest.

"This captain was coming down the dyke and he had men behind him. They were sweeping through and we were hovering a matter of feet away from them. I could see this clearly, and he emptied his clip into her."

Thompson said later, "I could hardly believe

what I saw. It was not a matter of interrogation. It was not a threatening move. He just shot a defenseless, wounded person."

Shortly afterward, Thompson pulled back and circled over My Lai Four again.

"We went over the area and looked down at the rubble and mess below, the people dead, and we saw a little boy lying next to a ditch. He was bleeding badly, but he was alive.

"We marked the spot with smoke again. This time a lieutenant stepped up with a rifle in hand, aimed it at the kid and emptied his clip into the kid.

"That happened a third time with a child and then again with a woman.

"We saw this one woman hiding there. She was alive and squatting. She looked up when we flew over. We dropped a smoke marker.

"When we came back she was in the same position, only she was dead. The back of her head was blown off. It had to be point-blank," said Colburn.

All the while the fury had been building inside Thompson. He was angry when he saw the first incident, but he knew no one had control of the situation when he saw it was happening over and over again.

It became obvious that the operation had gone completely mad, that there was no real officer in

charge of the situation and that if he didn't do
something it might spread throughout the area.

Thompson knew that innocent people were being
killed. Something had to be done. And quickly.

He tried to get ground troops on the horn, but
that didn't work.

He radioed reports of what was happening back
to his brigade headquarters.

Other helicopters were monitoring the messages
sent and received. And obviously Lt. Col. Frank
Barker caught the message in one of them.

At that time Barker called from his helicopter to
Medina on the ground.

Medina said he had a body count of 310. "I don't
know what they're doing. The first platoon's in the
lead. I am trying to stop it," he said.

Then Medina radioed Calley and said, "That's
enough for today."

Another witness with Calley, according to
Seymore Hersh, had a different story. He said,
"Medina called Calley and said, 'What the fuck is
going on?' Calley said he got some VC, or some
people that needed to be checked out." Then
Medina told Calley to have his men save their ammunition.

However, according to other witnesses in the
area, this particular conversation had occurred an
hour earlier. By about 10:30 a.m. Medina told

Calley, "That's enough for today," and made it a direct order.

"But Calley didn't stop," said Sledge. "That was when the incident at the second drainage ditch started.

"That's when he tried to get Maples to join in the shooting and he wouldn't do it. I turned away too, did something else."

As Thompson told of his ordeal later: "I kept flying around and across a ditch that had a bunch of bodies in it and I didn't know how they got in the ditch. But I saw some of them were still alive.

"I kept reporting back to headquarters what was going on. It was sickening. I wanted to do something to help."

Thompson lowered the chopper next to the ditch. He saw soldiers running back and forth. Occasionally one would push a civilian into the ditch.

The warrant officer asked one man what he could do to help the people. "He said the only way he could help them was to help them out of their misery."

And Thompson was up again.

But no more than a hundred yards away he saw a group of women and children, all of them obviously frightened, trying to hide and crouch together in a bunker next to another ditch.

He landed again.

"I don't know, maybe it was just my belief, but I hadn't been shot at the whole time I had been there and the gunships following hadn't.

"I had seen no one being fired at on the ground, and saw no signs of the enemy anywhere except that first armed man in the field as we were coming in.

"When I got out I saw the lieutenant (Calley), and some of the men who had killed the woman earlier, and the little boy.

"I asked him if he could get the women and kids out of there before they tore it up, and he said the only way he could get them out was to use hand grenades.

" 'You just hold your men right here, and I'll get the women and kids out,' I told him."

Colburn told it: "He told us that if any of the Americans opened up on the Vietnamese, we should open up on the Americans.

"He stood between our troops and the bunker. He was shielding the people with his body. He just wanted to get those people out of there."

Other larger helicopters had been called in, and they landed nearby.

Thompson gathered up two old men, two women and five children.

He put them into the waiting choppers, and one of the children died on the way to the Quang Ngan hospital.

Less than a half-hour later Thompson landed again. He had been looking down at the ditch filled with headless bodies, where blood flowed like a river from the many, many corpses, and as Varnado Simpson had said "he couldn't stand no more."

With Colburn along carrying a gun, Thompson waded knee-deep into the people and blood and picked up a little boy.

"He was still holding onto his mother. But she was dead," said Colburn later.

Thompson pried the child loose and carried him away from the huge grave.

"I don't think this child was even wounded at all, just down there among all the other bodies, and he was terrified," said Thompson.

He and his men flew the baby boy to the hospital.

Even the Army didn't want to give him credit. Sure, a medal.

But what caused them to make him be quiet?

Why didn't one official at Ft. Rucker or in the Pentagon answer simple questions about Thompson's heroics?

The Army knows the answer and has kept it locked within the system.

Thompson, the hero, is hushed while Calley, the criminal, makes headlines and news magazine covers. While the nation is shouting "Free Calley!" the populous has forgotten Thompson exists.

Chapter Twelve

After My Lai

"After My Lai Four there were dead people everywhere, piles of them scattered along the sides of the streets, pushed up against the sides of the concrete houses," said Calley.

"I saw a pretty little girl with big black eyes with a sort of page-boy haircut. Her brunette hair was cut in bangs, and it was immaculately combed.

"She was about three years old and as cute as she could be, dressed in a red dress and barefooted.

"I went over to her. I smiled and she smiled.

"I sat down beside her and took some cookies from my ration kit. I gave her some, and we ate them together.

"She didn't talk any. I don't think she was old enough to talk. I don't know. I do know that if her mother and father lived in the village, they died that day. And what bothers me more than anything is that the most horrible thing that has happened in that little girl's life is having to live through that day.

"Medics took her away, and I don't know what happened to her after that. I didn't try to find out. Hell, that was war—and it hurt."

The U.S. didn't win at My Lai.

Estimates have it that about 500 persons—South Vietnamese civilians—were actually killed during the two-day foray that continued into Pinkville and the surrounding countryside.

The day after Charley Company left My Lai Four, communist VC troops gathered the dead from the streets and held their own types of funeral services.

First Platoon, still led by Calley, did not turn back. They were going full speed ahead. They plowed into Pinkville and took it.

They killed there, but not as many as in the Song

My village complex.

"After the shooting all the villagers became Communists," said Nguyen Bat to reporter Hersh. Bat was one of the survivors. Before the massacre, he said, he was not a Communist; afterwards, he changed his mind.

Late in the day of the first assault or during the morning of the second day, they can't seem to remember which, four soldiers found a woman in the midst of a group of peasants.

"She was a voluptuous gal, really something, but only about 15 years old, and ready to be cut," one of the men said.

"We pulled her out and tore her blouse down around her shoulders.

"Her eyes, pretty like dark almonds, glared at us, and she shouted some shit, but we got our hands inside the blouse and took hold of some nice firm soft, really sweet titties.

"A couple of the other guys reached in and copped themselves a feel, too."

The soldier telling the story laughed at this point. He remembered that some people—mostly old

159

women and little children—were screaming and crying about a hundred feet away.

"But we kept on what we were doing, playing and having ourselves a little fun. It had been hard work all day, getting up early, not sleeping much the night before, traveling like crazy all day.

"She was a pretty little thing, and we told her so.

"One of the other guys said, 'Let's see what she's made of.'

"By that time we had the blouse damn near all the way off her.

"Another guy said, sort of giggling like, 'VC Boom-Boom,' that's whore, see.

"About that time one of the guys grabbed hold of another young girl, and they started in on her in the same way. She was just as pretty as the first.

"An old lady came out of the bunch and started raising all manner of hell, fussing and fighting and cussing.

"Somebody knocked the hell out of her with the butt of an M16, but we didn't let up with the gals. We were really getting worked up over ours, and we pulled her way back away from the group.

"The old lady was still giving the others hell. I think somebody finally said, 'Waste 'em,' but we weren't there then. We had our gal away from the others, back over in a field on the other side of a tall bunch of green shrubs or something. We heard some strong fire, but we didn't take our minds off what we were doing.

"That gal, she was the best we had had in such a long time. She even had pretty legs, I noticed when I got up off her. She was nice, really; not like some of those Saigon whores you get clap-clap from; she was sweet.

"I left when somebody else showed up and wanted to try it.

"Later I heard the fourth guy got pissed because she kept turning away. Somebody said that guy shot her." He made a pained face. "It was a damned shame, too."

When their march to the sea was over, and all behind them had been destroyed, Charlie Company was tired.

They were glad to get back to Dottie, where Medina told them not to worry about an investigation into the happenings of the past two days. He would fix anything that needed fixing, he said.

And they believed him.

Several days later was the first time Ronald Ridenhour saw the sight.

The village, looking down on it from a helicopter,

appeared desolate. There were no signs of life—no people.

Ridenhour, whose letters to congressmen more than a year later sparked the investigations which led to the eventual disclosure and courts-martial of principal figures, said that he saw a body from the helicopter.

As the copter flew lower, he saw that it was the body of a woman "spread-eagle as if on display. She had an 11th Brigade patch between her legs—as if it were some type of display, some badge of honor. We just looked. It was obviously there so people would know the 11th Brigade had been there. We just thought, 'What in the hell's wrong with these guys? What's going on?' "

"Calley was just as big of a sonofabitch after the slaughter as he had been before," said Sledge on reflection of his platoon leader.

"He never demanded any respect from any of us, before or after. He was a little punk bastard who didn't have a great deal of sense and who thought he was some kind of a big shot because he wore an Army uniform," said another.

"Who the hell would follow him into battle? I did, but I don't know why," came another comment.

Others had their complaints, and all said that none of the men were close to Calley.

It was not long before Calley was sent to another company, and finally on patrol duty behind-the-lines.

Chapter Thirteen

Soldier

When he was sent behind-the-lines he did his best to become a real soldier. Perhaps it was because of a guilt feeling, deep and unforgettable, left lingering in his soul from the My Lai nightmare.

"He seemed to take to the jungle like a duck to a pond," said one of the men who went on search-and-destroy missions with Calley in the highlands of Laos and Cambodia during the winter of 1968 and spring of 1969.

"After his time was up in Nam he signed up for an extra year. Maybe it was because he had found a home in the hills.

"If he hadn't he sure as hell acted like it. There was a girl up there he was friendly with. She was a guide, a good-looking but tough Laotian. She took us on a lot of the patrol missions to the villages in the northern country.

"Sometimes we'd have to be out two or three nights, and Calley had her in his sleeping bag. She was about his size, small, and maybe that's why he liked her so much.

"If you've ever seen the type you'd know her. She acted cold, like so many of the oriental types. She'd look at you with a blank stare, those pretty almond-shaped eyes just glaring sort of simple like. But she must have known what it was all about.

"She wore camouflage dungarees and Calley's paratrooper boots and carried an M16. And she knew how to use the rifle.

"One time we were up in the mountains and came on two snipers. Looked like for a minute they had us in a crossfire and were going to cut us down.

"We made it to cover because of her. She ducked like some kind of track star into some bushes and brought one of the sonsofbitches down.

"By that time we had made it to the trees, and we

kept the other monkey busy while she got back to us.

"She was something else, and she liked her little man an awful lot. You could see that by the way she acted toward him, bringing him food and fixing his hooch and slipping in with him at night."

Later Calley said, "Vietnam was not a bad place. Fact is, I liked it very much. I liked the people and the beautiful terrain."

It must have taken him a while, because he said when he first arrived at the Da Nang airport in December of 1967 he felt the harsh cold eyes staring at him and wondered what the people were thinking.

"One time I picked up an orphan and took her with me. This was after My Lai.

"She looked hungry and sad. She was about four or five years old, and I knew that I couldn't legally adopt her.

"I took her home to base camp with me anyway and fed her. She stayed at the camp about a month before I took her to one of the South Vietnamese orphanages.

"That night the VC came and killed everybody in the orphanage, including a priest and two sisters.

"The next day I went with the other soldiers and we buried about 30 children. We sent the bodies of the sisters to Germany and the padre to the United States. The father's head had been completely cut away from his body.

"I went in and did my job. I didn't even look for the little girl. I knew that some day I'd want to rationalize that she made it out of there.

"And after that I didn't look at children again. I didn't want to become attached to them. I didn't want to feel any love for them. I became uninvolved, so I couldn't get hurt."

"Lt. Calley found himself in the jungles," said one of the young man's superiors.

"He enjoyed that life as much as anybody I've ever seen, and I was connected with Merrill's Marauders during World War Two and I've seen many of 'em come and go. Calley wanted to stay over here where it's tough, where it's hard to survive and where it's an entirely different life from that back in the states.

"Personally, I think he should have been allowed to remain. The Army didn't have to court-martial him. That was something they did because of the pressure of the press. It was bullshit."

"That was my kind of Army," Calley later said about Company G, 75th Rangers, which was the Marauders during an early time.

168

"It's the real Army, the way I think of it. Those guys were warriors. They had shit in their greens. They were tough as hell. There were no civilians in that group, they were all soldiers, and they liked it. They had been trained to fight, and they knew how to fight as well as any professional soldier in the world. They never backed away. And with them, I had become totally committed to this kind of fighting."

But Calley was not allowed to remain in Southeast Asia.

On June 6, 1969, he was ordered home to Washington, D.C.

"I didn't have any idea why I was leaving," he said. "Hell, I thought maybe they wanted to decorate me or something."

He was to report to the Inspector General, and when he entered the offices was led to Col. W. V. Wilson, the officer who was leading the investigation into the My Lai incident for the IG.

In reply to Wilson's questions about civilians killed during Task Force Barker near Pinkville, Calley said, "I don't know what you're talking about."

"I was angry," Calley told a reporter later.

Wilson asked Calley if he had legal counsel.

Calley said, "I don't think I need a legal counsel."
Then Calley asked if the Army was planning to
prosecute him.

"He (Wilson) didn't answer my question, so I
asked about his investigation. He said that it was
possible that I might be charged with murder of
civilians in the Pinkville Operation as a result of
his investigation.

"He said that he was conducting the investigation
under the direction of the Chief of Staff."

Everything that both of them said was taken
down on a tape recorder.

Then Wilson began questioning Calley.

Calley gave him only his name, rank and serial
number. "I refused to answer any question, but I
told him that if he was trying to find our new and
better tactical changes for operations similar to the
Pinkville Operation, I'd be more than glad to help."

Wilson said that he was not looking into tactical
questions.

The colonel said he was investigating the operation and trying to find out if any civilians were
killed.

Calley told him, "I will not answer any questions
—unless I'm given a grant of immunity."

"We can grant no such immunity," Col. Wilson
said.

An Army legal officer was invited into the room

and said he would be Calley's attorney for the time being.

Then Wilson asked more questions.

And Calley again gave name, rank and serial number.

"The Army counsel actually did nothing but inform me of my rights. They already had him there for me, in case he was needed."

Calley stayed in a Washington hotel for two weeks. At the end of that time, after being questioned further by Wilson and others, he was reassigned to Ft. Benning.

"Even then I was pretty sick of all this. What the hell, when you're in Vietnam, when you're out there sweating your balls off, shooting and getting shot at, you think about getting back home where there's peace. I had been thinking that. I had been thinking about all the pretty girls who were waiting back home. I had been thinking about all the bullshit—mom and apple pie. But now I had none of that. I had been threatened with an investigation into a possible murder charge, and it made me have pretty bad nights."

Once during his two-week Washington stay he was put in a line-up. "They paraded me and four other guys—all of us in civilian clothes except one —before lights on a little narrow stage. We stood at attention and looked out toward the lights. I couldn't see what was on the other side of the lights, or who was out there. They didn't ask us any questions, and I don't know who was trying to identify us, or what they were doing. And I don't know what the outcome of it was, or anything else. It lasted about ten minutes.

"This only added to the way I had been feeling. As much as I tried to relax, I couldn't. More than before, it made me worried about the unknown. I guess that bothered me more than anything else. I didn't know what I had done wrong, so I didn't know how to defend myself," he said.

When he got to Benning he was assigned as an assistant instructor with the Ranger problems. About 50 miles south of the main post, still on the government land, he taught NCO students night patrolling and ambush techniques.

During these days Rusty Calley worked three or four days a week and was off three or four days. He and other junior officers took their outboards and girls to Lake Harding in Alabama and would spend weekends in lakefront cabins "and party it up something fierce."

"I really liked that job," he told a reporter. "It wasn't hard. We worked hard, then played hard. I lived in a house off post. I had plenty of dates. I met some real fine girls."

On Monday morning, September 1, 1969, five

days before his tour of duty was up, he was told by a colonel that he was to be transferred to the student brigade, 40 Company (Casual).

Calley was pissed. The last day of his regular tour was Saturday, and he had already decided he'd re-enlist. He wanted to make the U.S. Army a career.

"What did I do wrong?" he asked the colonel.

"Nothing. I have a good report on you from Ranger training."

"Well, what kind of job are you going to give me for one week?"

"You'll be assigned to the executive officer of 40th Company."

"I don't believe I'm being put there for that. That sounds ridiculous, assigning an officer to a different job on his last week in the service. There has to be more than that. What else do you know about my situation?"

The colonel said he knew nothing.

The last week was one of hell for Calley. He knew something was happening, but he couldn't put his finger on it.

In the meantime, a captain in the Airborne who had gotten into some trouble in the Dominican Republic recommended former Judge George W. Latimer as legal counsel, and Calley got in touch with him. Calley talked to him, told him the situation as he knew it and said he might need Latimer later.

On Wednesday, after several minor arguments with his CO in the Casual Company, Calley was assigned to Headquarters and Headquarters Company. His duty was to be an assistant personnel officer.

He didn't mind the job, but it bothered him that none of the officers had been around to see him about reenlisting. The last week was always one of red tape, filled with sales talks from recruiters who wanted the soldier to re-up.

Finally on Friday a major in charge of all reenlistments asked him if he would like to re-up.

"Can I?" asked Calley.

The major said, "That's not the matter at hand."

Calley then asked if he could get out of the Army.

The major asked if he wanted to stay in or get out.

Calley asked if the major knew anything about pending murder charges.

After a consultation with another party, the major asked the same question again.

Calley knew that he had not signed the correct papers, had not taken a physical and had been approached by no one else.

And from that moment on, throughout the day,

the Army kept a man with Calley. All officials knew that if he was not officially charged by the end of the day he could not be charged.

When Calley asked to consult his attorney, he was told, "This has nothing to do with your attorney."

The major said that he could get a warrant officer to walk Calley through the separation physical, if he desired.

Calley agreed.

As soon as he finished the physical, at about 4:30 p.m., he was taken to another colonel's office.

"I stood at attention before him. He had a sheet of paper in his hands while he sat at the desk.

"His face was like stone. He looked gray and solemn.

"He began reading the charges to me.

"Hell, I didn't know what to do or think," he said later, describing the situation to a reporter. "I had no idea the charges would be anything like this. He was reading something like 'not less than 30 nor more than 45,' 'not less than 20 nor more than. . . .' It all just escaped my mind at that time. Hell, I think I never thought at all. I just stood there and shit in my drawers."

The officer asked, "Do you understand these charges, Lt. Calley?"

Calley said, "Yes, sir. I understand, sir." He

saluted, turned and walked out of the office.

Outside the office another colonel took Calley to his office. "There is no need to publicize this thing," he said. "The U.S. Army won't publicize it, if you won't."

Calley agreed.

Back at his apartment he called Latimer and had several stiff drinks of bourbon.

Chapter Fourteen

Court-Martial

The court-martial of Lt. Calley was anticlimactic after the drama of the crime.

Like trials often are, it was filled with minute details, legalese jargon, verbal bouts between prosecution and defense attorneys.

Preceded by a series of preliminary hearings, point after point of contention was brought up by the chief defense counsel, George Latimer.

The most pertinent point was Latimer's attempt

to prove command influence in the actual decision to bring charges against Calley.

"The decision came from the highest rung in the ladder of the Army's system of command—the President of the United States," Latimer announced in the hearing before court-martial judge, Col. Reid W. Kennedy. "And I plan to prove that the order came down all the way to this post."

Although Latimer was allowed to parade several of Calley's former commanders and some of the brass from higher-up positions onto the witness stand, Kennedy over-ruled the counsel when he called Secretary of Defense Melvin Laird.

One of the commanders, Col. Jim K. Keirsey, testified during the hearings that he was ordered to "hold up" on the Calley prosecution at one time from a Washington leader.

Others from the Benning JAG office said that it had been a "touch-and-go" situation.

Kennedy ruled against Latimer's point of command decision.

Nevertheless, the point was made and will gain more prominence when the case goes into the appellate system.

And other points were made.

Not the least of these was Latimer's charge that his client was being unjustly held in the Army past his discharge date to face murder charges.

When he was formally charged, before the Article 32 investigation, Calley should have been a civilian, Latimer contended. The attorney said that Calley at that time was "not subject to the jurisdiction of any court-martial because he was not placed in jeopardy before the expiration of his initial term of service."

He was turned down by Kennedy.

But again he had made a point for possible appeal.

And later Latimer brought up contentions that questioned the entire system of military justice. The aging soft-spoken attorney charged that the court-martial is "constitutionally inferior to trial by jury," under decisions of the U.S. Supreme Court, and that it deprives an individual of constitutional rights.

Latimer argued that a trial by court-martial unnecessarily deprived Calley of equal protection of the law, including the right to be indicted by a grand jury and to be tried by a jury.

On each of these points Latimer was turned down by Judge Kennedy, but the sound of his voice and the meaning of his words were heard and understood around the world.

Latimer, during the hearings, reiterated what American Civil Liberties Union attorney Charles Morgan Jr. of Atlanta once argued eloquently while defending Dr. Howard Levy who had been court-martialed for refusing to train Special Forces medics. Morgan had stated that, "Justice in the military is, at best, an anomaly.

"Eventually," said Morgan, "the right to try military men, for all offenses, military and civilian, should be vested in the civilian courts, with civilian juries. Within the military, reform is almost like trying to reason with Attila the Hun."

Morgan had continued, "There's just no way of having any sort of trials conducted within the military. The military is incapable of understanding the Constitution.

"It is not by great acts but by small failures that freedom dies. The sense of justice dies slowly in a people. They grow used to the unthinkable and sometime they may look back and even wonder when 'things' changed. They will not find the day or a time or a place.

"Justice and liberty die quietly because men first learn to ignore injustice and then no longer recognize it. Once militarism captures the mind of a people, it spreads slowly—it is endemic; it moves undramatically. Unless military incursion on civilian life is stopped at constitutional walls, our nation and the world may go with either a bang or a whimper. But it will matter little, for freedom will have fallen not under a conqueror's heel but less gloriously—it will simply have marched away to a cadence count," Morgan wrote in his massive Levy brief.

Later the Army prosecutor in the Calley court-martial, Aubrey Daniel, would have his chance to speak of military justice.

Calley told a reporter, "I wanted to stay in the Army. If I could stay with the Rangers.

"And too, I wanted to clear myself of any accusations made by the Army.

"The last thing I wanted to do was get in the civilian court with a bunch of crying mothers—people who didn't know or care anything about combat."

But Calley did not understand the workings of the law nor the widespread implications of his case. He did not realize the actual situation he was confronted with at that time.

For four and a half long, tedious, grueling months the six officers of the U.S. Army who had been chosen to sit on the jury of the court-martial listened to the detail-by-detail accounts of what happened in My Lai on March 16, 1968.

The six included five who had been veterans of Vietnam combat zones.

Four days were spent questioning 25 officers, and finally six were selected.

The only man who had never been to Vietnam was heavy-set Col. Clifford H. Ford, a round-faced, graying veteran of many fronts in World War Two. The oldest of the jury, he marched into the courtroom with a chest filled with ribbons. A native of Knoxville, Tennessee, he was 53 years old.

As an enlisted man serving in the infantry, Major Charles C. McIntosh was wounded twice during battles in the Korean War. In the mid-fifties he became an officer, and during a skirmish in Vietnam he was again wounded. Twice, the 38-year-old native of Donora, Pennsylvania, won the Silver Star, and he too had many other decorations.

Major Harvey G. Brown, bespectacled and sporting an English-styled short-clipped mustache, was promoted from captain during the court-martial proceedings. Thirty-seven years old, he had served as an adviser to a South Vietnamese fighting unit in combat. He was a native of Amarillo, Texas.

Thirty-six-year-old Major Carl R. Bierbaum was the most youthful looking of the group. A native of Litchfield, Illinois, he served two tours of duty in Vietnam as a combat operations officer.

Captain Ronald D. Salem, a tall raw-boned westerner from Sioux Falls, South Dakota, had been a platoon leader in a combat zone in Vietnam. He was 34 years old.

Major Walter D. Kinard of Columbus, Georgia, had received the Silver and Bronze Star during combat in Vietnam. He was 33 years old.

After listening to five members of Calley's First Platoon testify for the prosecution as well as the testimony of Calley himself and Capt. Ernest Medina, a decision was reached.

Many technical witnesses had taken the stand and had offered testimony.

Calley and Medina's testimony, as seen in Chapter Ten, was conflicting. Someone was lying, and the jury had to determine which one.

Also, five of the members of First Platoon had testified against their leader, Calley. Each gave his own candid eye-witness account of the happenings of the day. And each was pointedly against the lieutenant.

For two weeks the jury stayed sequestered in the privacy of a conference room in the courthouse on Ft. Benning.

Twice records had been made. The court-martial had been the longest in history. And the deliberation was the longest.

183

On a warm Monday afternoon, March 29, 1971, little more than three years after the My Lai incident had occurred, Rusty Calley was fetched by his young deputy military defense counsel, Capt. Brooks Doyle Jr.

Calley had been taking a nap in his lush bachelor's apartment on the post—a new apartment from the one he had had one year and a half earlier when the charges were first brought against him. He had felt the prosperity of becoming a nationally known figure—a hero—and he had a color television and an expensive padded bar furnished with the best of whiskeys. He even had a private secretary, Mrs. Shirley Sewell, a pretty brunette, who answered the thousands of letters he had received since first making headlines.

"They've got the verdict," Doyle told Calley, who had put on nearly 20 pounds during the year and a half wait from the first charge to the final sentencing. He no longer looked like a school boy. He had grown paunchy. His face was wider, his eyes droopy.

Calley muttered, "So they're finally ready."

In his well-furnished bedroom, he quickly slipped into his Army greens.

A half-hour later he was standing before the court-martial.

At 4:30 p.m. Judge Kennedy asked the jury foreman, Col. Ford, "Have you reached a verdict?"

"We have, your honor," said Ford.

Sgt. Jefferson Huggins, a bailiff, took the sealed envelope from Ford and handed it to Kennedy.

The Judge ripped open the top of the envelope, read its contents—all the while his face remained emotionless and his lips did not move—then gave it back to Huggins.

Huggins returned the envelope to Ford.

"Col. Ford, will you rise and read the verdict," Kennedy said.

Calley stood in front of the jury box, facing Ford. Latimer flanked him on the right and his military attorney Major Kenneth Raby, stood to the left.

"We find the defendant guilty. . . ." Ford began.

Motionless, Calley listened to the words and watched the colonel's lips moving.

He had been found guilty of killing one person at the intersection of a trail, 20 at the ditch on the eastern side of My Lai Four and a man dressed in white. He was also found guilty of assaulting a two-year-old child.

As soon as Ford finished reading the verdict, Latimer rushed his client out of the courtroom and into a defense conference room.

After a short meeting, Calley was escorted to the nearby stockade by military guards.

After his client was locked up, Latimer said, "Take my word for it, the boy's crushed."

The lawyer said the verdict was "tragic and horrendous."

The 70-year-old attorney with wrinkled brow and soft gray eyes said, "This boy's a product of a system, a system that drug him up by the roots, took him out of his home community, put him in the Army, taught him to kill, sent him overseas to kill, gave him mechanical weapons to kill, got him over there and ordered him to kill."

The jury remained away from any contact with the public.

The following day Calley made his "You stripped me of my honor" speech while standing as straight as possible before the half-dozen who would decide whether he would receive life imprisonment or death.

Also, it was pointed out by Latimer that if the jury became hung up on which sentence to impose they might reconsider the original verdict and come up with a lighter verdict.

As soon as Calley finished, the 29-year-old prosecuting attorney, Aubrey M. Daniel III, who had handled the case with emotionless but superb candor, who had become obsessed with presenting a fair case with fact-speaking witnesses, took the floor and spoke out against the defendant.

Daniel's voice rose only slightly as he said, "You did not strip him of his honor." He turned and stared into the face of Calley.

"What he did stripped him of his honor. It never can be honor to kill unarmed men, women and children."

And he pivoted back to face the jury again. "We know that you will arrive at an appropriate sentence," he added.

Early Wednesday afternoon the jury had decided what to do with Calley.

The tight-lipped jury looked on the young officer as he stepped forward and snapped his customary salute.

At 2:32 p.m. Ford began reading the sentence.

Calley listened to the words "confined at hard labor for the length of your natural life" and did not take his eyes from Ford's lips.

In three days he would be shipped to Ft. Leavenworth, Kansas, where he would be confined to the disciplinary barracks for at least ten years, at which time there was the possibility for parole.

187

The defendant was ordered dismissed from the U.S. Army, his insignia stripped from his uniform, and his $773.10 per month pay forfeited.

All rights as a former serviceman would disappear.

Appeal of the sentence is automatic, but even the first level of the appeal system would take at least one year, according to Latimer.

Appeal time could go on for five years or longer, he added.

"I had the choice of two evils," Latimer said. "I got the lesser of two evils. I'd say Calley feels the same way."

The chief defense counsel said, "I'm confident the sentence will be abated."

And he added, "You'll find no case in military justice has torn America apart like this case has torn America apart."

Chapter Fifteen

Hero

America came alive, screamed and shouted, cried and sang out. The conscience of the country could not and would not accept the verdict.

Within days *Newsweek* and *Time* magazines came out with cover stories on Calley. It was their second time to give him covers inside of a two-year period. On the cover of *Newsweek*, above a photograph of Calley and a background photo of the dead victims of My Lai, was the legend: "Calley

Verdict: Who Else Is Guilty?" *Time's* cover had a drawing of Calley with the legend: "Who Shares the Guilt?"

One year and a half before the country had been stunned at the fact that a soldier could possibly be responsible for the mass slaying of innocent civilians—especially small children.

The people of the United States had been shocked in November of 1969 to discover that the Army would allow anything as horrible as My Lai to take place.

Now suddenly the blame was being lifted off of Calley. He was a mere victim. Several senators, including John Sparkman of Alabama, proclaimed Calley a "scapegoat." Others said he should be lauded rather than punished.

A spokesman for the American Legion in Columbus, Georgia, said that his group would raise $100,000 for a Calley defense fund "or die trying."

"We'll stand up and make ourselves be heard around the world if necessary," the spokesman proclaimed. "We've jailed an innocent boy while the culprits of the world roam the streets.

"Who are the murderers? Not people like Lt. Calley. He was only doing his duty.

"The real murderers are the demonstrators in Washington who disrupt traffic, tear up public property, who deface the American flag.

"Lt. Calley is a hero. He's an all-American. He fought for us in a country where communism is still trying to take over.

"We should be proud of him. We should elevate him to saint rather than jail him like a common criminal."

Words similar to these heard at a Legionnaire rally were spoken throughout the country.

And even Nixon reported that he received more than 100,000 letters and telegrams within 24 hours, and 100 to one called for the release of Calley.

Small town businessmen, politicians, former servicemen and others circulated petitions to be sent to the President asking for immediate pardon.

Hundreds of thousands of "Free Calley" bumper stickers were printed, sold, distributed and displayed within 24 hours after the sentence was announced.

In the Columbus, Georgia, Memorial Stadium, during a revival there, the Rev. Michael Lord told his congregation, "There was a crucifixion 2,000 years ago of a man named Jesus Christ. I don't think we need another crucifixion of a man named Rusty Calley."

As soon as the sentence was announced a recording company in Nashville headed by entrepeneur Shelby Singleton released a 45 rpm single entitled "The Battle Hymn of Lieutenant Calley." In the background was "The Battle Hymn of the Republic," and words were spoken by a disc jockey from Russellville, Alabama.

The record which begins, "My name is William Calley, I'm a soldier of this land; I've vowed to do my duty and to gain the upper hand; but they've made me out a villain, they have stamped me with a brand. . . ." sold more than 200,000 the first day of release.

It reached the million mark by Wednesday of the following week.

On Wall Street, John Kerry, a Silver Star winner from the Vietnam War, read a prepared statement as the spokesman for the Vietnam Veterans Against the War.

Kerry read, "We are all of us in this country guilty for having allowed the war to go on. We only want this country to realize that it cannot try a Calley for something which generals and Presidents and our way of life encourage him to do. And if you try him, then at the same time you must try all those generals and Presidents and soldiers who have part of the responsibility. You must in fact try this country."

Audie Murphy, the movie star who killed more than 200 Germans during World War Two and who later wrote about it in an autobiography, *To Hell*

And Back, said he was "distressed and shocked" at the Calley verdict.

"There have been My Lais in every war. Now for the first time we have tried a soldier for performing his duty," said the national commander of the Veterans of Foreign Wars, Herbert Rainwater.

Radio stations throughout the nation played "The Battle Hymn of Lieutenant Calley" incessantly, and followed it with requests for money for the Calley defense fund.

It was reported by one group that more than ten million persons had signed a petition protesting the conviction.

In response to the national appeal, Nixon made an unprecedented move Thursday evening, little more than 24 hours after the pronouncement of sentence had been made by Ford.

Calley was freed from the Ft. Benning stockade by Presidential order.

Pending appeal of his conviction, the 27-year-old, slightly overweight, balding and not so boyish lieutenant marched to an awaiting car with his single "light guard" who would accompany him day and night.

The guard was assigned to share Calley's bachelor quarters.

Until the appeals were completed, Calley would be restored to his rank and his salary.

The guard at his side, Calley was free to come and go as he pleased for work and laundry and business or legal conferences. He was ordered to make no public statements and never leave Ft. Benning.

White House authorities said the President had acted on his "own initiative," but it was plain that public opinion had swayed the Commander-in-Chief to intervene. He had, in effect, proclaimed Calley a National hero.

On hearing Nixon's decision, the House of Representatives applauded.

Herbert Rainwater said, "We are indeed grateful that the President has listened to the heartfelt pleas of our countrymen."

The following day Gov. George Wallace of Alabama, himself a candidate for the Presidency on a third party ticket in 1968, visited with Calley in his quarters for 13 minutes.

Wallace, who was in Columbus to address an American Legion fund-raising rally for Calley, told the press when he left Calley's apartment, "I believe President Nixon is going to do the right thing and the right thing is to grant clemency to Lt. Calley.

"I would call on the President and the Congress and I think they will respond, not to me but to the American people."

After all, Calley was now a hero—and you don't imprison heroes.

Chapter Sixteen

Daniel

If there was a star of the Calley court-martial it was Captain Aubury M. Daniel III, the prosecutor for the U.S. Army.

A man for all seasons, a moralist, a pragmatic young lawyer who never knows when to stop—only when the job is completed—Daniel is a Virginian who loves the law as many men love some prized ideal.

"He becomes absolutely involved with a case,

and there's nothing stopping him then," said a colleague recently.

Daniel certainly became involved with the Calley case and took it seriously. For more than a year it filled his entire schedule at Ft. Benning.

Medium height, as trim as a welterweight in shape, the owner of a winning smile and a prophetic, resounding voice, the 29-year-old Daniel was born in a small town in South Carolina named Moncks Corner. He was raised, however, in Orange, Virginia, about 70 miles west of Richmond.

He graduated from the University of Virginia and took his law degree from the University of Richmond.

Following a year of private practice in Arlington, Daniel was drafted. While in basic training at Ft. Dix, New Jersey, he received a direct commission and became an Army attorney.

Capt. Bruce Shreves, a colleague at Ft. Benning, told *New York Times* reporter James T. Wooten, "Like everything else he has ever done, he's been completely immersed in the Calley case.

"He's so damn good that I believe if he'd been defending Calley, the verdict would have been different."

During the court-martial Daniel never sought publicity. Whenever asked questions by newsmen, he answered wryly, "No comment."

Like most Southern lads, he liked to tip the bottle on occasion, according to friends. But not during the Calley trial. Throughout the tedious time he lived and breathed his work, with no diversions.

After the President decided to release Calley to his quarters, Daniel came out in the open for the first time.

Daniel, whose only ambition is to be a trial lawyer in civilian life and who had less than a week left in his four-year tour of duty, was obviously disheartened at the President's decision.

He sat down and wrote the following letter, which says as much about the law in this case as anything else ever published:

"Sir:

"It is very difficult for me to know where to begin this letter as I am not accustomed to writing letters of protest. My only hope is that I can find the words to convey to you my feelings as a United States citizen, and as an attorney, who believes that respect for law is one of the fundamental bases upon which this nation is founded.

"On November 26, 1969, you issued the following statement through your press secretary, Mr. Ronald Ziegler, in referring to the My Lai incident:

" 'An incident such as that alleged in this case is in direct violation not only of the United States military policy, but is also abhorrent to the conscience of all the American people.

" 'The Secretary of the Army is continuing his investigation. Appropriate action is and will be taken to assure that illegal and immoral conduct as alleged be dealt with in accordance with the strict rules of military justice.

" 'This incident should not be allowed to reflect on the some million and a quarter young Americans who have now returned to the United States after having served in Vietnam with great courage and distinction.'

"At the time you issued this statement, a general court-martial had been directed for a resolution of the charges which have been brought against Lieutenant William L. Calley Jr. for his involvement at My Lai.

"On December 8, 1970, you were personally asked to comment on the My Lai incident at a press conference. At that time you made the following statement:

" 'What appears was certainly a massacre, and under no circumstances was it justified.

" 'One of the goals we are fighting for in Vietnam is to keep the people from South Vietnam from having imposed upon them a government which has atrocity against civilians as one of its policies.

" 'We cannot ever condone or use atrocities against civilians in order to accomplish that goal.'

"These expressions of what I believe to be your sentiment were truly reflective of my own feelings when I was given the assignment of prosecuting the charges which had been preferred against Lieutenant Calley. My feelings were generated not by emotionalism or self-indignation but by my knowledge of the evidence in the case, the laws of this nation in which I strongly believe, and my own conscience. I knew that I had been given a great responsibility and I only hoped that I would be able to discharge my duties and represent the United States in a manner which would be a credit to the legal profession and our system of justice.

"I undertook the prosecution of the case without any ulterior motives for personal gain, either financial or political. My only desire was to fulfill my duty as a prosecutor and see that justice was done in accordance with the laws of this nation. I dedicated myself totally to this end from November of 1969 until the trial was concluded. Throughout the proceedings there was criticism of the prosecution but I lived with the abiding conviction that once the facts and the law had been presented there would be no doubt in the mind of any reasonable person about the necessity for the prosecution of this case and the ultimate verdict. I was mistaken.

"The trial of Lieutenant Calley was conducted in the finest tradition of our legal system. It was in every respect a fair trial in which every legal right of Lieutenant Calley was fully protected. It clearly demonstrated that the military justice system which has previously been the subject of much criticism was a fair system. Throughout the trial, the entire system was under the constant scrutiny of the mass media and the public, and the trial of Lieutenant Calley was also in a very real sense the trial of the military judicial system. However there was never any attack lodged by any member of the media concerning the fairness of the trial. There could be no such allegation justifiably made.

"I do not believe that there has ever been a trial in which the accused's rights were more fully protected, the conduct of the defense given greater latitude, and the prosecution held to stricter standards. The burden of proof which the Government had to meet in this case was not beyond a reasonable doubt, but beyond a possibility. The very fact that Lieutenant Calley was an American being tried for the deaths of Vietnamese during a combat operation by fellow officers compels this conclusion.

"The jury selection, in which customary procedure was altered by providing both the defense and the prosecution with three peremptory challenges instead of the usual one, was carefully conducted to insure the impartiality of those men who were selected. Six officers, all combat veterans, five having served in Vietnam, were selected. These six men who had served their country well, were called upon again to serve their nation as jurors and to sit in judgment of Lieutenant Calley as prescribed by law.

"From the time they took their oaths until they rendered their decision, they performed their duties in the very finest tradition of the American legal system. If ever a jury followed the letter of the law in applying it to the evidence presented, they did. They are indeed a credit to our system of justice and to the officer corps of the United States Army.

"When the verdict was rendered, I was totally shocked and dismayed at the reaction of many people across the nation. Much of the adverse public reaction I can attribute to people who have acted emotionally and without being aware of the evidence that was presented and perhaps even the laws of this nation regulating the conduct of war.

"These people have undoubtedly viewed Lieutenant Calley's conviction of an American officer for killing the enemy. Others, no doubt out of a sense of frustration, have seized upon the conviction as a means of protesting the war in Vietnam.

"I would prefer to believe that most of the public criticism has come from people who are not aware of the evidence, either because they have not followed the evidence as it was presented, or having followed it they have chosen not to believe it.

"Certainly, no one wanted to believe what occurred at My Lai, including the officers who sat in judgment of Lieutenant Calley. To believe, however, that any large percentage of the population could believe the evidence which was presented and approve of the conduct of Lieutenant Calley would be as shocking to my conscience as the conduct itself, since I believe that we are still a civilized nation.

"If such be the case, then the war in Vietnam has brutalized us more than I care to believe, and it must cease. How shocking it is if so many people across the nation have failed to see the moral issue which was involved in the trial of Lieutenant Calley —that it is unlawful for an American soldier to summarily execute unarmed and unresisting men, women, children and babies.

"But how much more appalling it is to see so many of the political leaders of the nation who have failed to see the moral issue or, having seen it, to compromise it for political motive in the face of apparent public displeasure with the verdict.

"I would have hoped that all leaders of this nation, which is supposed to be the leader within the international community for the protection of the weak and the oppressed regardless of nationality, would have either accepted and supported the enforcement of the laws of this country as reflected by the verdict of the court or not make any statement concerning the verdict until they had had the same opportunity to evaluate the evidence that the members of the jury had.

"In view of your previous statements concerning this matter, I have been particularly shocked and dismayed at your decision to intervene in these proceedings in the midst of the public clamor. Your decision can only have been prompted by the response of a vocal segment of our population, who while no doubt acting in good faith, cannot be aware of the evidence which resulted in Lieutenant Calley's conviction.

"Your intervention has, in my opinion, damaged the military judicial system and lessened any respect it may have gained as a result of the proceedings.

"You have subjected a judicial system of this country to the criticism that it is subject to political influence, when it is a fundamental precept of our judicial system that the legal processes of this country must be kept free from any outside influences. What will be the impact of your decision upon the future trials, particularly those within the military?

"Not only has respect for the legal process been

205

weakened and the critics of the military judicial system been given support for their claims of command influence, the image of Lieutenant Calley, a man convicted of the premeditated murder of at least 21 unarmed and unresisting people, as a national hero has been enhanced, while at the same time support has been given to those persons who have so unjustly criticized the six loyal and honorable officers who have done this country a great service by fulfilling their duties as jurors so admirably.

"Have you considered those men in making your decision? The men who since rendering their verdict have found themselves and their families the subject of vicious attacks upon their honor, integrity and loyalty to this nation.

"It would seem to me to be more appropriate for you as the President to have said something in their behalf and to remind the nation of the purpose of our legal system and the respect it should command.

"I would expect that the President of the United States, a man whom I believed should and would provide the moral leadership for this nation, would stand fully behind the law of this land on a moral issue which is so clear and about which there can be no compromise.

"For this nation to condone the acts of Lieutenant Calley is to make us no better than our enemies and make any pleas by this nation for the humane treatment of our own prisoners meaningless.

"I truly regret having to have written this letter and wish that no innocent person had died in My Lai on March 16, 1968. But innocent people were killed under circumstances that will always remain abhorrent to my conscience.

"While in some respects what took place at My Lai has to be considered to be a tragic day in the history of our nation, how much more tragic would it have been for this country to have taken no action against those who were responsible.

"That action was taken, but the greatest tragedy of all will be if political expediency dictates the compromise of such a fundamental moral principle as the inherent unlawfulness of the murder of innocent persons, making the action and the courage of six honorable men who served their country so well meaningless."

Thus Daniel not only proved himself as a courtroom performer, he showed himself to have the courage of his convictions.

Meanwhile, the jurors shook their heads with dismay at the indignation of a country.

"It had to be done," said Major McIntosh.

Others backed up the statement.

"I don't think that there was any other verdict we could have reached," said Major Kinard. "We looked for anything that would prove Lieutenant Calley innocent. We gave Lieutenant Calley every benefit of the doubt."

"I wanted to believe it didn't happen, that it was a hoax," said Major Brown. "I'll have to live with this verdict the rest of my life."

Perhaps the juror most sympathetic toward Calley was Major Bierbaum. He said, "I think ten years would be justice. I don't mean parole in two years. I mean ten years confinement." That is exactly what the life sentence does; it allows the possibility of parole after ten years.

Chapter Seventeen

Press

The news media responded quickly to the Calley situation, to the verdict, the sentencing and President Nixon's action.

Hundreds of editorials and outspoken columns were published taking both the pro and con side of the coin.

News analysts weighed the social and moral and legal questions brought to the surface by the court-martial and its decision.

As Latimer had predicted, "No case in military justice has torn America apart like this case has torn America apart."

And to take his statement one step further: no criminal or civil case in the courts of this country had been so closely followed or had such far-reaching results.

At the close of the trial, William Greider, a brilliant reporter with *The Washington Post,* wrote an article headlined "The Moral Question and Battlefield Laws." He had covered the court-martial from the outset. He had reported the events of the four and a half months with an objective, observant eye.

After Calley's release from the stockade following the public's loud clamor, Bill Greider wrote, "Americans have chosen some strange popular heroes in the last decade, but none of them was a convicted mass murderer."

He reminded the public that Calley was "the guy, remember, who was held responsible by a jury of his peers for 'wasting' 22 lives. He picked up a baby, threw him into a ditch and shot him. He is the soldier who butt-stroked an old man in the face, then shot him at point-blank range and blew away the side of his head. Some hero."

Greider continued, "The question is: if the President and the nation reject the verdict of guilty, rendered by six combat veterans, what is left of the law which the Army attempted to uphold—the international covenant that, even in combat, soldiers do not shoot defenseless people who are captured and unarmed?

"If that principle is undone by the public uproar over Calley's conviction, the Army is stuck with a different kind of problem: should it give up the battlefield discipline required by U.S. law and the Geneva Convention? Should it open the doors at Ft. Leavenworth, Kan., and release all the other soldiers convicted of the same offense as Calley?

"Contrary to popular belief, Calley is not the first American soldier prosecuted for killing people in the middle of this war. There have been scores of men—soldiers and Marines—tried for the murder of Vietnamese captives in the midst of combat situations. Many of them are still in prison. The only difference is that, instead of 22 people, most of them killed only one or two."

"Right now, there are 75 to 80 men serving time in Ft. Leavenworth on murder charges which originated in Vietnam. Some of their victims were fellow Americans, but most were Vietnamese. Some of them, just like Calley, still have their appeals pending. Still more are imprisoned at the Naval Prison in Portsmouth, New Hampshire, where convicted Marines are sent.

211

"They're sitting in prison unknown while Lt. Calley is famous and confined to his quarters on post."

The Wall Street Journal handled the matter similarly in an editorial: "The spectacular public reaction to the Calley conviction is easily understandable, but there comes a time when the nation needs to get its feet back on the ground. This is a young man duly convicted of taking unarmed prisoners entirely at his mercy, throwing them in a ditch and shooting them. Is this nation really to condone such an act, as a strange coalition of superpatriots and peace marchers seems to urge?"

Samuel C. Brightman, former deputy chairman of the Democratic National Committee and a former Army officer, wrote in *The New York Times,* "I know that war—all war—whatever ugly adjective the doves apply to Vietnam as though it were the first and only 'immoral' war. I know that Lieutenant Calley will be a scapegoat, albeit a murderer, if the investigation stops with him or with Captain Medina. A scapegoat, a victim, a weakling, an unfit soldier gobbled up by an army desperate for manpower and turned into an officer because he had gone to military school long enough to pass that key Army aptitude test of knowing his left foot from his right foot—maybe all of these, but a hero? No!"

The Sunday Star of Washington, D.C. published

an editorial following the Calley release and ended it by stating that, "the day this country goes on record as saying that unarmed civilian men, women and children of any race are fair game for wanton murder, that will be the day that the United States forfeits all claims to any moral leadership of this world. We do not believe that black day has come."

And perhaps, out of all the hundreds of thousands of words written, James Reston, columnist for *The New York Times*, put it down at his sarcastic best. On April 4 he wrote, "For a while it almost looked as if somebody were going to propose giving Lieutenant Calley the Congressional Medal of Honor. Not since the firing of Gen. Douglas MacArthur during the Korean war has there been such an outburst of sympathy for an American soldier. So at last Vietnam has produced an officer everybody recognizes—an anti-hero for a war without glory or nobility and a symbol for a time of moral confusion."

Chapter Eighteen

Limbo: II

Today only grown-up children play war games.

Little boys and girls do not put on daddy's Army greens and pretend they are soldiers in Vietnam. The war itself is too close.

Every afternoon before dinner one can watch the real thing taking place on the screen of the television, and that alone is enough to keep one from the battlefields of the empty lot next door. All of the romantic imaginings of a child's mind have been drained from the idea of shooting the enemy.

Because of the horrible day of chaos in a village named My Lai Four perhaps the United States will pull out of Vietnam quicker than it would have without such a reminder that war is hell.

The decision to put Rusty Calley behind bars for life was too much of a shock to the common man in the United States. Men and women of middle America saw their own sons being locked up. They could not abide to see such a thing happen.

In retrospect, it is my wish that these people will want to look into what caused My Lai Four. Why did "good American boys" commit such acts? What is the weakness in our own system—social or military—that allowed such an atrocity to take place?

If we look into the psychological and social background of it, hopefully we will find a cure for our own ills. Hopefully we will be a better nation filled with better people.

I do not dislike Rusty Calley for what he did. I feel sympathy toward him and the other officers in that long chain of command.

Perhaps Rusty Calley is only a scapegoat. No matter, we do know, as Capt. Daniel stated so beautifully and powerfully in his letter, that the facts show he did kill and he did assault. Do we allow

216

this to continue to happen? When it does happen, do we leave it unpunished?

A lawyer friend of mine, a moralist, a former infantryman and a present active reserve officer, said sarcastically, "Boys will be boys." He added later, a crooked smile on his sardonic lips, "If you've got a lot of ammunition, why waste it?"

Unfortunately this has been the serious attitude of too many military leaders in this country's history. But these leaders seem to forget that the people back home nowadays are very much a part of war. No longer can they send their dispatches home with one-sided reports. Today we sit in our easy chairs and we have a ringside seat to bloody battles only hours after they have taken place— and we can witness for ourselves the hell of war.

While Calley grows fat in his small apartment on the grounds of Benning, other men are wondering how to use him.

For most of his life Calley has been a pawn in the hands of better men, more powerful men and sometimes wiser men.

During those early months of 1968 while he was being psyched into putting the rush on the Song My villages and Pinkville he was a pawn in the hands of the Army.

Immediately over him was "Mad Dog" Medina, an ambitious Captain who wanted to make a name for himself in Vietnam. He had never had the book-learning necessary to become a major, so he had to prove his worth on the battlefield.

Lt. Col. Frank A. Barker Jr. was the commander of the entire Task Force, the three companies, Alpha, Beta and Charlie, whose mission it was to take the communist stronghold seaport.

Barker, who was later killed in a helicopter crash in Vietnam, directed the operation.

Above Barker was Col. Oran K. Henderson, the commander of the 11th Infantry Brigade, who was charged with covering up the massacre originally.

Others up the ladder of the chain of command include Major General Robert E. Cushman Jr., commanding general of the Third Army; Gen. William C. Westmoreland, commander of the U.S. troops in Vietnam; Adm. U.S. Grant Sharp, commander-in-chief of the Pacific Command; Gen. Earle G. Wheeler, chairman of the Joint Chiefs of Staff; Secretary of Defense Clark M. Clifford, and U.S. President and Commander-in-Chief of all U.S. military Lyndon B. Johnson.

In one way or another, all had their hand on the little fellow who was nothing but a movable chess piece.

Later Calley became a pawn again when he was put on trial to save the U.S. Army for its sins.

"He gave his only begotten son. . . ."

Calley loved the U.S. Army, and he knew that the Army would take care of him. Never would the father turn on his son.

But someone had to be sacrificed. The life of an institution was at stake. And when this occurs, you do not go to the lowest man on the totem pole. You can't go to an enlisted man, a poor weakling who is too much a part of the people. That would be too easy.

To wash its own soul clean of guilt the institution must turn to one of its bright young men, one of its potential leaders, just as the pagan religions annually sacrificed the brightest and most handsome young male before the crucifixion of Christ, who was a symbol of all such sacrifices. With this type of belief instilled into its collective mind, the U.S. Army pointed its finger at Calley.

Again he was the pawn.

Now he has been released into limbo by a President who became afraid of the loud outcry of the populous. Calley was carried from the punishment of hell and placed in an in-between waiting area.

This time he was a political pawn and will remain such a pawn for as long as the politicians seek to use him, then he will be allowed to rot uselessly in limbo.

Nixon has already used Calley to appease the American public. He has even announced that he will have the final say-so in the case, but didn't bother to announce that he has the last word because that is military law. One would think that he decreed it such.

And within hours after Nixon put Calley back into his apartment on the Army post, Alabama Gov. George Wallace visited him.

After their conversation, Wallace gave a news conference outside the apartment and said that Nixon should do the right thing and release Calley.

Later that night at a "Free Calley" rally Wallace told the group that he had changed his mind about the Vietnam War. He said that while he preferred victory, he thought the U.S. should immediately withdraw all troops from Southeast Asia. He even gave the peace sign.

Obviously he had heard the whisper of the crowd. He had seen the tide of opinion shift. He's a master at recognizing such, and he's a master at moving his pawns wherever he wishes.

On the day after Wallace's speech, my writer friend, William Bradford Huie, who has been after the Third Party candidate for the Presidency since Wallace first won the gubernatorial race on a racist platform in 1962, wrote Calley a letter giving advice.

"Dear Lieutenant Calley:

"As a citizen and as a journalist I am one of your supporters. I want to see you freed, either by the Army, the Congress or the President. One development, however, concerns me, and I understand that it is worrying you and your attorney. I refer, of course, to George Wallace's attempt to take you over and use you for his purposes.

"Now, you and I and your attorney know that Wallace can't help you: he can only hurt you. Because he's a racist. He won the Alabama governorship in 1970 by the thinnest of margins only by shamefully appealing to the prejudices of poor white men against poor black men. He is held in contempt by four out of every five Americans.

"Wallace fouls every well from which he drinks. Four Southern governors were invited to the rally in your behalf at Columbus. When the other three governors learned that, Wallace spoke to a half-filled auditorium. That rally wasn't a success; it was a failure because Wallace tried to turn it, not to your advantage but to his. There isn't a governor in the United States, and there aren't ten members of

Congress, who will willingly appear on any platform with Wallace. He stands alone as a hateful and hate-filled opportunist supported by an insignificant minority of Negro-hating white men and women.

"Now in private you have made clear that you are not a Wallaceite. So most certainly you must not allow Wallace to alienate the millions of Americans, across the broad spectrum, who now support you but who despise him.

"You must not delay. Promptly and publicly you must disown Wallace. You must not permit him to visit you again, and you must inform him publicly that while you appreciate his being one of your supporters you are not and never intend to be one of his."

But Calley did not divorce himself from Wallace, and the man who will be running for the Presidency in 1972 on the American Independent Party ticket continued to make Calley a political issue.

From the inside circles of the national Wallace For President headquarters in Montgomery the word had it that one of Calley's defense attorneys, Richard B. Kay of Cleveland, Ohio, has his eye on the vice presidential nomination with Wallace.

222

Kay, who entered the Calley case without fee, was an American Independent Party official in Ohio during the national election of 1968. He obtained a good deal of exposure during the court-martial, and his name could keep Calley alive as a political issue in the 1972 election.

And thus Calley continues to be maneuvered by the people in positions of authority.

If President Nixon released him from all custody tomorrow, giving him a full pardon, Calley would remain in limbo.

In the outside world today he would be a pawn in the hands of economic wolves. Already public relations representatives are preparing worldwide speaking tours in which he will state his religious philosophy as well as his belief that peaceful living is better than war. Already these hungry dogs are writing his speeches, telling him how he must act, and they are even sending ministers to visit him while he is in his apartment awaiting an outcome of his appeal.

And as soon as they have drained all the usage out of him, the hounds of the greenback will toss him into limbo again.

His fate has already been tarnished, and he will remain in limbo.

Acknowledgements

There are so many, many people who have contributed to this book that it is almost impossible to sit down and acknowledge them all—but I will try.

Thanks first of all should be given to my editor and publisher at the *Alabama Journal*, Harold E. Martin, who has been mentor and inspiration to many young Southern reporters in the past few years. He allowed me to take the time to explore the Calley story in the very beginning.

Appreciation is also in order to the other editors on the *Journal*: Ray Jenkins, Ben Davis, Joe McFadden and Bernie Kuhl, as well as to all my fellow staff members who helped in their own valuable ways.

Other newsmen, such as Jack Nelson with the *Los Angeles Times* and Jim Wooten of *The New York Times*, gave encouragement and advice along the way.

225

Thanks are added to my friends in the Pentagon who were shocked at what they discovered in the records and who wanted to make the facts public.

I am appreciative of the help given by some of the members of Charlie Company who talked as freely as possible under the circumstances—as well as others who knew and know Rusty Calley.

My close friend, Tom Cork, an editorial writer for the *Journal* and a sharp analyst of the news scene, gave assistance in the preparation of the manuscript and talked until the early hours of many mornings about the situation.

Others who helped in their own fine ways were: U.S. Rep. William L. Dickinson, his staff and especially Walter Bambert; Charles Morgan, Jr. Ira DeMent, George Seitz, Sam Stephens, Don Ragsdale, Tom Ray, Warner Stough and others.

Last but not least, thanks are offered to my wonderful friends, George and Jane Dean, whose patience and hospitality during the writing of this book was greatly appreciated.

Wayne Greenhaw
West Egg Two
Destin, Florida
May 14, 1971

Recognition is given to Seymour Hersh's "My Lai 4" published by Random House.